KASHMIR SHAIVISM

The Secret Supreme

KASHMIR SHAIVISM

The Secret Supreme

SWAMI LAKSHMAN JEE

SRI SATGURU PUBLICATIONS
A DIVISION OF
INDIAN BOOKS CENTRE
DELHI-INDIA

Sri Satguru Publications
A Division of
Indian Books Centre
24/4, Shakti Nagar, Near Dena Bank,
Delhi-110007

India

First Indian Edition : 1991

ISBN   81-7030-257-9

PRINTED IN INDIA

GUIDE TO PRONUNCIATION

T he following English words exemplify the pronunciation of selected Sanskrit vowels and consonants.
The Romanized Sanskrit vowel or consonant is first list-
ed and then a English word is given to aid you in its
proper pronunciation.

a	as	**a** in **A**merica.
ā	as	**a** in f**a**ther.
i	as	**i** in f**i**ll, l**i**ly.
ī	as	**i** in pol**i**ce.
u	as	**u** in f**u**ll.
ū	as	**u** in r**u**de.
ṛi	as	**ri** in mer**ri**ly.
ṛī	as	**ri** in mar**i**ne.
e	as	**e** in pr**ey**.
ai	as	**ai** in **ai**sle.
o	as	**o** in st**o**ne.
au	as	**ou** in h**ou**se
ś	as	**s** in **s**ure.
ṣ	as	**s** in **sh**un , bu**sh**
s	as	**s** in **s**aint, **s**in

PREFACE

T his book consists of lectures that I delivered in
1971–1972. It began in 1969 when Maharṣi Mahesh
Yogī came to our Valley. He had heard of me and wanted
to meet me so he called on me. When he visited me he
asked if I would speak to his disciples and I agreed. He
then sent his transport and I was taken to where he was
staying with his Western disciples. When I arrived there
was a huge gathering of Western devotees waiting for
me. I spoke to them giving a discourse on important
points in Kashmir Śaivism.

John and Denise Hughes were also present in that
gathering, but at that time I had not yet met them. They
must have been impressed with what they heard for in
1971 they returned to Kashmir and came to see me at my
Āshram. I asked them who they were? They said they
were Maharṣi's disciples. They then explained to me that
they had heard my discourse when they first came to
Kashmir with Maharṣi in 1969. John then told me that he
had one problem, he wanted to learn Kashmir Śaivism
and would I have time to teach him? I replied, "yes, I
have enough time." I instructed him that he should come
to the Āshram on the next Tuesday and I would begin
teaching him. So on Tuesday he arrived, along with his
tape recorder, and I began giving him lectures in the

Āshram hall. Denise his wife also attended these lectures.

In the beginning I taught John only the introductory topics of Kashmir Śaivism. As time passed, however, I came to know that John had good power of understanding and I became fond of him. I wanted to tell him more and more about Kashmir Śaivism, to teach him Śaivism's secrets, so I continued giving lectures and John recorded them. This was the main starting point of his studies. It is these secrets, these major points which I taught him at that time, which comprise this book.

As I appreciated that John was assimilating the lectures very well, after they were completed I started teaching him the theory which is found in the Śaiva scriptures. In this manner Kashmir Śaivism was taught to him.

I think when these lectures are printed it will be a great boon for mankind and will elevate the whole world. Also, I will consider myself blessed by Lord Śiva. I hope that John will continue writing on what I have delivered to him in theory and practice — *the Secrets Supreme*. If he continues to expose it to the world it will be a great help for everyone.

Swami Lakshman Jee

TABLE OF CONTENTS

PREFACE
INTRODUCTION

Chapter One   **1**
    Thirty Six Elements
      Tattvas

Chapter Two   **11**
    The Six Fold Path of the Universe
      Ṣaḍadhvan

Chapter Three   **15**
    The Theory of the Alphabet
      Mātrikācakra

Chapter Four   **29**
    The Theory of Reflection
      Pratibimbavādaḥ

Chapter Five   **33**
    The Explanation of the Means
      Upāyas

Chapter Six   **41**
    The Theory of Speech
      Vāk

Chapter Seven   **47**
    The Three Impurities
      Malas

Chapter Eight   **51**
    The Seven States of the
    Seven Perceivers *(Pramātrin)*

Chapter Nine   57
The Seven Processes of the
    Seven Perceivers *(Pramātṛin)*

Chapter Ten   65
The Five Great Acts of Lord Śiva
    Pañcakṛityavidhiḥ

Chapter Eleven   71
The Five States of the Individual
    Subjective Body

Chapter Twelve   87
The Five Fold Contacts of Masters
    and Disciples

Chapter Thirteen   89
The Manifestation of the Tantras

Chapter Fourteen   97
Mokṣa in Kashmir Śaivism and
    Indian Philosophy

Chapter Fifteen   103
Kashmir Śaivism and Advaita
    Vedānta

Chapter Sixteen   109
Seven States of Turya

Chapter Seventeen   119
Kuṇḍalini and Its Purpose

Chapter Eighteen   127
Variations in the Rise of
    Prāṇa Kuṇḍalini

Chapter Nineteen   131
Kashmir Śaivism

INTRODUCTION

Due to events of the past the tradition and teachings of Kashmir Śaivism have remained concealed for the past eight hundred years. Swami Lakshman Jee is the last and the greatest of the Saints and Masters of this tradition. He is like a splendid and rare jewel. He has spent his whole life, beginning when he was a small boy, studying and practicing the teachings of this tradition and in so doing has, due to his intellectual power and the strength of his awareness, realized both spiritually and intellectually the Reality of its thought.

In his teachings he constantly emphasizes the secular nature of this great tradition. He wants it to be clearly understood by everyone that Kashmir Śaivism does not discriminate against anyone on the basis of caste, creed, colour, or sex. No one is restricted from involving his or herself in the practice and teachings of this tradition. This teaching is a universal teaching open to one and all.

The secret keys necessary for unlocking the treasury of knowledge which Kashmir Śaivism embodies has, since ancient times, been passed verbally from Master to disciple. It is this oral tradition which is the very life of this teaching and it is Swami Ji who is the last living depository of this secret wealth. He is very concerned, therefore, that the reality of this tradition and teaching is

Chapter One

Thirty Six Elements

Tattvas

To begin with I will explain to you the nature of that which is known as the *tattvas* or elements. In Vedānta we are told that there are only twenty five *tattvas*, however, in Śaivism we know that there are really thirty six *tattvas*. These thirty six *tattvas* are the most important points for entering into Śaivism.

I will give the explanation of the *tattvas* in the way of rising not coming down. We must rise up to *Parama Śiva*. I like rising, I do not like coming down, so we must rise. I will, therefore, explain the grossest element 'earth' first and then proceed to explain subtler and subtler elements until we reach the subtlest element, the finest, which is *Parama Śiva*.

THIRTY SIX TATTVAS—36 ELEMENTS

Pañca mahābhūtas—Five Great Elements

pṛithvī	=	earth
jala	=	water
tejas	=	fire
vāyu	=	air
ākāśa	=	ether

Pañca tanmātras—Five Subtle Elements

gandha	=	smell
rasa	=	taste
rūpa	=	form
sparśa	=	touch
śabda	=	sound

Pañca karmendriyas—Five organs of action

upastha	=	creative
pāyu	=	excretion
pāda	=	foot
pāṇi	=	hand
vāk	=	speech

Pañca jñānendriyas—Five Organs of Cognition

ghrāṇa	=	nose, organ of smelling
rasanā	=	tongue, organ of tasting
cakṣu	=	eye, organ of seeing
tvak	=	skin, organ of touching
śrotra	=	ear, organ of hearing

Antaḥkaraṇas—Three Internal Organs

manas	=	mind
buddhiḥ	=	intellect
ahaṁkāra	=	ego connected with objectivity
prakṛti	=	nature
puruṣa	=	ego connected with subjectivity

Ṣaṭ kañcukas—Six Coverings

niyati	=	limitation of place
kāla	=	limitation of time
rāga	=	limitation of attachment
vidyā	=	limitation of knowledge
kalā	=	creativity
māyā	–	illusion of individuality

Śuddha tattvas—Pure Elements

śuddha vidyā	=	Iness in Iness—Thisness in Thisness
īśvara	=	Thisness in Iness
sadāśiva	=	Iness in Thisness
śakti	=	Iness
śiva	=	Iness (Being)

We will begin, therefore, from the lowest degree of the *tattvas*, which are the gross *tattvas*. The gross *tattvas* are called the *pañca–mahābhūtas,* the five great elements. They are the *tattvas* of *pṛithvī* (earth), *jala* (water), *tejas* (fire), *vāyu* (air), and *ākāśa* (ether). The element 'ether' is not a perceptible element such as the elements 'earth', 'air', 'fire', and 'water'. Rather, it is space, unoccupied space. It gives you room to move. It is that element in which the other four gross elements have room to exist. We could say that it is a special vacuum which is filled by the other four great elements. These *tattvas* are gross and are called *mahābhūtas* (great elements) because the whole universe is based on these five elements.

After the five *mahābhūtas* you move up to the five *tanmātras.* The five *tanmātras* correspond to the five *mahābhūtas. Gandha tanmātra* arises from the element of earth (*pṛithvī tattva*). the word '*gandha*' means smell, however, it is not exactly smell, it is the abode of smell, where smell lives. And that abode of smell is called *ganda tanmātra*. The next *tanmātra*, *rasa tanmātra*, has come out from the element of water *(jala mahābhūta)*. *Rasa tanmātra* is the residence of the impression of taste *(rasa)*. And then from the element of fire *(tejas mahābhūta)* issues forth *rūpa tanmātra*. Though the word '*rūpa*' means form, *rūpa tanmātra* is not exactly form, it is the residence of form, where the impression of form resides and this residence is called *rūpa tanmātra*. From the element of air *(vāyu mahābhūta)* rises *sparśa tanmātra* which is the *tanmātra* of touch, the sensation of touch. This *tanmātra* is the residence of the sensation of touch. And finally, rising from the element of ether *(ākāśa mahābhūta)* is *śabda tanmātra*, the *tanmātra* of sound. This is the residence of the sensation of sound.

After the five *tanmātras* comes out the five *tattvas* which are known as the five *karmendriyas*, the five organs of action. These organs of action are *vāk, pāṇi, pāda, pāyu,* and *upastha*. The first *karmendriya* is *vāk tattva*, the organ of speech. Next is *pāṇi tattva*. The word '*pāṇi*' means hand. *Pāṇi* is that organ of action, by which you take and give. Then comes *pāda tattva*. The word '*pāda*' means foot. It is the organ by which you move about. It is the organ of locomotion. Next is *pāyu tattva* which is the active organ of excretion. It is the organ of passing stools. The fifth and last *karmendriya* is *upastha tattva*. *Upastha tattva* is that *karmendriya*, that organ of action, which is the active organ of sex. It is the organ of sex and the organ of urination, the organ by which sex is performed and by which one urinates.

The next five *tattvas* are the five organs of cognition, the five organs of knowledge, and are known as the five *jñānendriyas*. These are the mental organs with which we experience the world. These five organs are *ghrāna, rasanā, cakṣu, tvak,..,* and *śrotra*. The first *jñānendriya* is *ghrāna tattva*. The word '*ghrāna*' means nose. The use of the word 'nose' does not refer to breathing, rather 'nose' is used here to indicate smell. This is the organ of cognition by which you smell. It creates odours. The next *tattva* is *rasanā tattva*. *Rasanā* means tongue. Here the use of the word 'tongue' does not refer to speech but to taste because, though speech also comes from the tongue, it is an organ of action not an organ of cognition. *Rasanā tattva* is that organ of cognition by which you taste. It creates flavours. Now follows *caksu tattva*. The word '*caksu*' means eye. It is that organ of cognition by which you see. It creates form (*rūpah*). The fourth *jñānendriya* is *tvak tattva*. *Tvak* means skin. It is the organ of cognition by which you feel. It creates touch. The last organ of cognition is *śrotra tattva*. *Śrotra* means ear. It is that organ of cognition by which you hear. It creates sound.

All of the above twenty elements; the five *mahābhūtas*, the five *tanmātras*, the five *karmendriyas*, and the five *jñānendriyas*, are called gross elements. They are all objective elements. The following elements, as we continue rising in our explanation of the *tattvas*, are said to be objective cum subjective elements. You should understand though, in Śaivism all the elements are really objective elements. They are called objects. Only that Super Being is subjective. Yet, as the following elements are a bit more attached with subjectivity than the former, we say that they are objective cum subjective elements.

Now we rise to the three *tattvas* which are known as the *antahkaranas*. The word '*antahkaranas*' means internal organs. The three internal organs are *manas* (mind), *buddhih* (intellect), and *ahamkāra* (ego).

Manas tattva, the element of mind, is said in Sanskrit to be '*samkalpasādhana*', the means by which you create thought. This could be any thought such as, "I am going there, I will go there, I have done this, I have done that". This is the action of *manas.* The action of *buddhiḥ tattva,* the element of intellect, is to confirm whether I should do this or not. This is the field of the confirmation, of the rightness of any proposed action whether intellectual or moral, because, first you must determine the rightness of a proposed decision or action and then make a choice dependent on this rightness. You ask yourself internally, "should I do this action or not, is this the right decision or not?" The *buddhi* will reply to you, "no, you should not do it", or "yes, you should do it." "This is bad, it is wrong to do it." "This is good, you should do it." "This answer is right, this answer is wrong." All this is done by the intellect.

Ahaṁkāra tattva is the element of ego which is connected with objectivity. When you attribute any action or knowledge to your own self such as, "I have done this and it was a mistake, I have done that and I ought not to have done it", or "I did a wonderful thing today which will benefit me a lot", this is the action of *ahaṁkāra tattva.* It creates limited 'I' consciousness, the limited ego which is connected with objectivity.

Rising still further we come to the two *tattvas* of *prakriti* and *puruṣa.* These two *tattvas* are interdependent. *Prakriti* is dependent upon *puruṣa* and *puruṣa* is dependent upon *prakriti.* *Prakriti* is the element which is referred to and is known as 'nature'. It is the field where the three tendencies arise and flow forth. These three tendencies are known as the three *guṇas,* the three qualities. They are respectively *sattva, rajas,* and *tamas.* *Prakriti* is the combination of these three *guṇas* but without any distinction. The three *guṇas* come out from *prakriti* and thus it is said that the three *guṇas* are not in the field of the *tattvas.* They are not to be considered as *tattvas* because they are created by *prakriti.* *Tattvas* are creators, they are not created. It is, therefore, not the *guṇas* which are *tattvas* but their creator *prakriti.* And that which responds to that *prakriti,* which owns that *prakriti,* is called *puruṣa.*

Up to this point I have explained twenty five *tattvas;* five *mahābhūtas,* five *tanmātras,* five *karmendriyas,* five *jñānendriyas,* three *antahkaranas, prakriti,* and *purusa.* This is the limit of the *Vedāntin's* understanding of the *tattvas.* They say that there are only twenty five *tattvas.* Yet in Śaivism nothing as yet has happened. All of these *tattvas* exist in the field of *māyā,* in the field of objectivity.

In Śaivism, *purusa* is not a realized soul. *Purusa tattva* is bound and limited just as *ahamkāra tattva* is. The only difference that exists between *purusa* and *ahamkāra* is that *purusa* is connected with subjectivity and *ahamkāra* is connected with objectivity. And this *purusa* is entangled and bound in five ways which are the five *kañcukas niyati, kāla, rāga, vidyā,* and *kalā.*

First there is *niyati tattva.* The function of *niyati tattva* is to put the impression in *purusa* that he is residing in such and such a particular place and not in all places. You are residing in a houseboat near first bridge and you are not residing simultaneously at Ishiber near Nishat. You are residing in Kashmir, you are not residing simultaneously in Australia or Canada. This is the limitation which *niyati tattva* causes for *purusa;* that he is residing in such and such a particular place and not everywhere.

Next comes *kāla tattva.* The word 'kāla' means time. The action of *kāla tattva* is to keep *purusa* in a particular period. He becomes the victim of being in a particular period. For instance, you are twenty five years old, I am sixty four years old, and he is forty three years old. This limitation is the result of the action of *kāla tattva.*

The third *tattva* by which *purusa* is limited is known as *rāga tattva.* 'Rāga' means attachment. This is that attachment which results from not being full. The action of *rāga tattva* is to leave the impression in *purusa* that he is not full, that he is not complete, and that he must have this and that to become full. As he does not have this he must have it to be full. He feels a lacking which he must fill. This is the function of *rāga tattva* in limiting *puruṣa*.

The fourth *tattva* which limits *puruṣa* is *vidyā tattva*. 'Vidyā' means knowledge. The action of *vidyā tattva* is to put the impression in *puruṣa* that he has this or that particular and limited knowledge, that he is not all knowing for he knows only some limited things.

The fifth and final bondage and limitation for *puruṣa* is *kalā tattva*. *Kalā tattva* creates the impression in *puruṣa* that he has some particular creativity, some particular artistic talent. He has mastered the art of writing, or the art of music, or the art of medicine, however, he does not have unlimited creativity. He is good at some things and not all things.

These five bondages of *puruṣa* are caused by *puruṣa's* ignorance of his own nature. And this ignorance is another *tattva* which is known as *māyā tattva*. These five *tattvas* are created by *māyā* for *puruṣa*. That *puruṣa*, therefore, who is the victim of *māyā*, does not know his own real nature and becomes bound and entangled by these five *(kañcukas)* and thus becomes a victim of *prakṛti*. He takes on individuality and becomes a limited individual.

These five *tattvas* plus *māyā* are six *tattvas* which are known as *ṣat kañcukas* (the six fold coverings). These are the six coverings which bind and entangle and, therefore, limit *puruṣa*. He is not limited by only one covering but by six coverings and these coverings must be removed, uncovered, and this is done automatically by the grace of the Master. Through this grace, at the time of real knowledge, *māyā* is transformed into His *śakti*, His great energy. In His glory *māyā* becomes the glory of *Parama Śiva*. When *puruṣa* realizes the reality of his nature, māyā becomes glory for him.

We have completed our examination of those *tattvas*, from the *antaḥkaraṇas* to *māyā*, which are connected with objectivity cum subjectivity. We will now rise to those *tattvas* which are connected with subjectivity, pure subjectivity. This is the subjective course to be entered into by *puruṣa* for rising, for rising from pure subjectivity to purer subjectivity to purest subjectivity.

Pure subjectivity is found in the *tattva* known as *śuddhavidyā tattva*. This exists when *puruṣa* actually realizes his own nature. And yet that realization is not stable, it is flickering, it is moving. This is the realization at the level of *śuddhavidyā tattva*. This realization is in movement. Sometimes you realize it, sometimes you forget it. And the experience (*parāmarśa*) of *śuddhavidyā tattva* is, "I am *śiva*, this universe is in duality. This universe is unreal, I am *śiva*." This is the impression which comes in *śuddhavidyā tattva* and it is pure subjectivity.

Now purer subjectivity will come in the next two *tattvas*, *īśvara tattva* and *sadāśiva tattva*. In *īśvara tattva* you realize, "This universe is my own expansion. This universe is not an illusion, it is my own expansion." This is the realization which takes place in *īśvara tattva*. The realization which takes place in *sadāśiva tattva* is the same as the realization which takes place in *īśvara tattva*, however, it is more refined. In *sadāśiva tattva* you realize, "I am this whole universe." This is the difference between these two impressions. In *īśvara tattva* you have the impression, "This universe is my own expansion," whereas in *sadāśiva tattva* you will find "I myself am this whole universe. Oh myself, I am this whole universe." These two *tattvas* comprise subjectivity in a purer form.

Now in the final two *tattvas* we come to subjectivity in its purest form. These two *tattvas* are the interdependent *tattvas*, *śakti tattva* and *śiva tattva*. The impression which comes in these two *tattvas* is only I, the pure I, the universal I. It is not the impression 'this universe is my own expansion' or 'I am this whole universe', no, it is just I, pure I, universal I.

Last is that Being which does not come in the cycle of

tattvas. That Being is called *Parama Śiva*. *Parama Śiva* is not only found in *śiva tattva* or in *śakti tattva*. It is not only here, It is not only there, everywhere you will find It. You will find It from the lowest *tattva* to the highest *tattva*. It is all levels, that is why It is no level. It is everywhere, that is why It is no where. The one Being who is everywhere, It is no where.

Chapter Two

The Sixfold Path of the Universe
Ṣaḍadhvan

In Śaivism this objective universe is said to be threefold because it is composed of three paths *(adhvans)*. These *adhvans* are said to be gross *(sthūla)*, subtle *(sūkṣma)*, and subtlest *(para)*. The gross path is called *bhuvanādhva*, the subtle path *tattvādhva*, and the subtlest path *kalādhva*—first *bhuvanādhva*, then *tattvādhva*, and finally *kalādhva*.

The word *'adhvan'* means path. Here path has a two fold meaning, it is either that path on which you tread, or that path which you must dispose of, you must discard. Either you have to tread on the path or you have to discard the path. You can dispose of this path only by the grace of your Master. And when you dispose of this path you reach the state of *Parama Śiva*.

There is no question of realizing God through treading on this path. Let you tread for centuries and centuries and still you will be treading. So, you must discard this path, dispose of it. When you do dispose of the path that is also called *adhvan*. Disposing of the path, however, can only be done by the grace of the Master who is the embodiment of *Parama Śiva*.

That path which is said to be gross is known as *bhuva-nādhva*. *Bhuvanādhva* means the path of all the worlds. In Śaivism these worlds are said to number one hundred and eighteen. By one world I do not mean one planet. This whole cosmos including suns, moons, stars, and planets is called one world. It has been found by yogins in *samādhi* that there are one hundred and eighteen worlds like this cosmos or world which have been created. This combination of one hundred and eighteen worlds is called *bhuvanādhva*.

The complete system of the thirty six *tattvas*, which I have explained earlier, is called *tattvādhva*. *Tattvādhva* means the course of all elements, the path of the *tattvas*. This is that path which is subtle.

That path *(adhvan)* which is more refined than *tattvādhva* is known as *kalādhva*. It is said to be that path which is subtlest. *Kalādhva* consists of five *kalās* which are five boundaries or enclosures. These *kalās* are enclosures for all of the thirty six elements, the thirty six *tattvas*, from earth up to Śiva. The first and outermost enclosure is called *nivritti kalā*. In *nivritti kalā* you will find the first *tattva*, *prithvī tattva*, the element 'earth'. The next *kalā* or enclosure is called *pratisthā kalā*.

"pratisthā avyakta gocare"

In *pratisthā kalā* you will find existing the twenty three *tattvas* from *jala tattva*, the element 'water', up to and including *prakriti tattva*. The next enclosure is known as *vidyā kalā*. *Vidyā kalā* contains the seven *tattvas* from *purusa tattva* up to and including *māyā tattva*. The next enclosure is called *śāntā kalā*. *Śāntā kalā* contains the four *tattvas* from *śuddhavidyā tattva* up to and including *śakti tattva*, the thirty fifth *tattva*. The fifth and last enclosure is known as *śāntātītā kalā*. Here, you will only find the existence of *śiva tattva*.

This course of the three fold *adhvans* is called *vācyādhva*. The word '*vācya*' means that which is observed, spoken, told. So *vācyādhva* is the path of that which is observed, seen, realized. It is called *vācyādhva* because it is seen, it is observed, it is created, it is felt. It is the objective cycle of this creation.

Now, we must turn to its observer, the creator of this *adhvan*. The creator of the three fold path of the universe known as *vācyādhva* is called *vācakādhva*. The meaning of the word '*vācaka*' is that which observes, sees, and creates. And so that path which observes, sees, creates, is called *vācakādhva*. It is the subjective cycle of this creation. And, like *vācyādhva*, *vācakādhva*, being composed of three paths, is also three fold. These paths are gross *(sthūla)*, subtle *(sūkṣma)*, and subtlest *(para)*.

Gross *(sthūla)* *vācakādhva* is called *mantrādhva* and consists of sentences because sentences are said to he gross. Subtle *(sukṣma)* *vācakādhva* is called *padādhva* and consists of words because words are known to be more subtle than sentences. Subtler than *padādhva*, the world of words, is the path of letters called *varṇādhva*.

Take any object such as a pot. That object will come in the three fold world of *vācyādhva*. It is an offshoot of the thirty six elements. On the other hand, the word 'pot' is *vācakādhva* for this object. So, this object is *vācya* and its *vācaka* is the word 'pot'.

The combination of all of these six *adhvans*, the totality of the three objective *adhvans* and the three subjective *adhvans* is called *ṣaḍadhva*, the six fold *adhvans*. This is the explanation of this whole universe, both subjective and objective.

Chapter Three

The Theory of the Alphabet
Mātṛikācakra

Mātṛikācakra is the theory of the alphabet. This theory teaches us that this whole universe is created by God, Lord Śiva, as one with, and not separated from, His own nature. He has created this universe in His own Self as the reflection of His sweet will. The creation of this universe is the outcome of this reflection. In Śaivism the sweet will of God is known as *icchā śakti*, the energy of will. It is through His will that the reflection of the universe takes place in His own nature. This reflection, however, is not like that reflection which takes place in an ordinary mirror wherein the mirror is the reflector and that which is reflected in the mirror is external to the mirror. The reflection of the universe, which takes place in Lord Śiva's own nature, is like the reflection which takes place in a cup shaped mirror. Here Lord Śiva takes the formation of a cup and puts another cup in front of His nature. And in that second cup, which is inseparable from Him, the reflection of the universe takes place.

This universe, as I explained earlier, is contained in the thirty six elements, the thirty six *tattvas* . And from the point of view of descending, first comes *śiva tattva*, then *śakti tattva*, then *sadāśiva tattva*, then *īśvara tattva*, then *śuddhavidyā tattva*, then *māyā tattva*, and so forth. Yet the reflection of the universe does not take place in this descending manner, from *śiva tattva* to *śakti tattva*, to *sadāśiva tattva*, to *īśvara tattva*, etc. Rather, it takes place in a reverse fashion. The reflection of the universe takes place from *prithvī tattva*, the element earth, to *śakti tattva*, from the lowest to the highest, not from the highest to the lowest. Just like in the ordinary course of experience when you see your face in a cup shaped mirror, your head will appear as down and your body will appear as up. In the same way this whole universe begins from *śakti tattva*, but it is experienced as beginning from *prithvī tattva*. The lowest element earth is reflected first and then the element water, then fire *(agni)*, then air *(vāyu)*, and so on up to *śakti tattva*.

And so, even though the real way in which the universe is expanded is from *śiva tattva* to *śakti tattva* and so on, this reflection makes you feel as if the lowest element earth is reflected first. And this is due to the fact that it is reflected. It is the reflection that makes you feel in this way because this reflection is an inseparable reflection. There is no mirror outside which is separate from that which is reflected in the mirror. In the ordinary course of experience you experience that which is reflected in the mirror is at one place and the mirror, which is the reflector, is at another. In the reflection of the universe, however, the reflected and the reflector are inseparable. It is Śiva and His Śakti, the energy holder and His energy, His energy of will.

Lord Śiva, the reflector of this whole universe, is full of five energies, and these five energies are *cit śakti*, the energy of consciousness, *ānanda śakti*, the energy of bliss, *icchā śakti*, the energy of will, *jñāna śakti*, the energy of knowledge, and *kriyā śakti*, the energy of action.

These five energies are represented in the sixteen vowels of the Sanskrit alphabet, "a, ā, i, ī, u, ū, ṛi, ṛī, li, lī, e, ai, o, au, ṁ, h", which sixteen vowels comprise *śiva tattva*.

The first letter of the Sanskrit alphabet, "a", represents *cit śakti*, the energy of consciousness of Lord Śiva. The second letter of the Sanskrit alphabet, the letter "ā", represents *ānanda śakti*, the energy of bliss of Lord Śiva. *cit śakti* and *ānanda śakti*, the energies of consciousness and bliss, are totally inseparable. Where there is consciousness *(cit)* there is bliss *(ānanda)*, and where there is bliss there is consciousness. Here, at this stage, the universe has not yet taken its shape. It is only residing in *ānanda śakti*, the energy of bliss.

After *cit śakti* and *ānanda śakti* comes *icchā śakti*, the energy of will. *Icchā śakti* is represented by the third and fourth letters of the alphabet, the letters "i" and "ī". You must understand that *icchā śakti* is not desire it is will. It is a wrong understanding to think of *icchā śakti* as the energy of desire. It is not the energy of desire, it is the power of will. And this *icchā śakti* takes two forms, unagitated *icchā śakti* and agitated *icchā śakti* . In its unagitated form, *icchā śakti* resides peacefully in its own nature and is represented by the letter "i". Next the agitated formation of *icchā śakti* takes place. This state is represented by the next letter of the alphabet, the letter "ī". This is the state of agitated will. In this state Lord Śiva's will is agitated but not in such a way that it is separated from His own nature. It remains as residing in His own consciousness and bliss, *cit* and *ānanda*.

At this point the apprehension takes place in Lord Śiva's consciousness that if I go forward, if I move onwards I may loose my own nature. And this apprehension takes place in *jñāna śakti*, the energy of knowledge, of Lord Śiva and is represented in the next two letters of the alphabet, the letters "u" and "ū". The first of these two letters, the letter "u", is called *unmeṣa*. The word *unmeṣa* indicates that the universal existence is about to begin, it is just forthcoming. It has not yet begun, it is not yet created, it is about to be created. And when He begins to create the universe He becomes apprehensive and this apprehension is known as *ūnatā* which means "lessening". This apprehension is represented by the letter "ū". It is that state in which Lord Śiva has the apprehension that His *cit śakti* and *ānanda śakti* may be decreased if He continues to move out to create the universe. This apprehension keeps Him at a stand still and prevents Him from moving forward.

He, therefore, discards the universe from His own nature. He separates the universe from His own nature and resides in His own *cit śakti* and *ānanda śakti*, consciousness and bliss. This state, wherein Lord Śiva has rejected the universe and is only residing in His own nature of consciousness and bliss, is represented by the next four vowels of the alphabet, the letters "ṛi, ṝi, ḷi, ḹi". The state that these four vowels indicate is that state where the Supreme, filled with consciousness and bliss, resides in His own nature. He does not move out. Because of this there is no possibility of the universe coming out into manifestation. The manifestation of the universe stops totally. Hence these four vowels, "ṛi, ṝi, ḷi, ḹi" are called *amrita bīja*, which means "residing in His own bliss *(ānanda)* ". At this stage there is no thought of creating the universe. These four vowels do not create anything. The state of Lord Śiva, which these four vowels represent is known as *anāśrita śiva*. *Anāśrita śiva* refers to that Śiva who has not accepted the existence of the universe in His own nature. He does not allow the universal existence in His own nature. In this state Lord Śiva resides in His own nature forever.

The apprehension, "If I create this universe I may loose My own nature," came out from the agitated will of Lord Śiva, from the agitated state of his *icchā śakti* . Yet the first two energies of Lord Śiva, *cit śakti* and *ānanda śakti*, the energies of consciousness and bliss, do not recognize this apprehension. These two energies are at ease. They understand that to create this universe is only the glory of His nature, therefore, why be apprehensive. There is no question of apprehension arising in Lord Śiva. Why, therefore, should He be frightened about coming out. Coming out or going in is the same thing to Him. As these two energies, *cit śakti* and *ānanda śakti*, have this understanding, therefore, they begin afresh to create this universe.

So *cit śakti* and *ānanda śakti*, the energies of consciousness and bliss, which are represented in the vowels "a" and "ā", create contact with *icchā śakti*, the energy of will, which is represented in the vowels "i" and "ī" and create the letter "e". And then simultaneously *cit śakti* and *ānanda śakti* contact "e" and give rise to the letter "ai". And when *cit śakti* and *ānanda śakti* come in contact with *jñāna śakti*, the energy of knowledge, which is represented in the letters "u" and "ū", they create the letter "o". And when simultaneously *cit śakti* and *ānanda śakti* contact the letter "o" they give rise to the letter "au". So when "a" or "ā" come in contact with "i" or "ī" the letter "e" is created. And when "a" or "ā" come in contact with the letter "e" the letter "ai" is created. In the same way when "a" or "ā" come in contact with "u" or "ū" the letter "o" is created. And when "a" and "ā" come in contact with "o" the letter "au" is created.

These four letters, "e, ai, o, au", which were created by the contact of *cit śakti* and *ānanda śakti* with *icchā śakti* and *jñāna śakti*, represent the four states of *kriyā śakti*, the energy of action of Lord Śiva. The first state of the energy of action, which is represented by the letter "e", is called *asphuṭa* (not vivid) *kriyā śakti* . In this state the energy of action is not clear. In the next movement and state of *kriyā śakti*, which is represented by the letter "ai", the energy of action becomes *sphuṭa*, vivid. In the third state of *kriyā śakti*, represented by the "o", the energy of action becomes *sphuṭatara*, more vivid. And in the fourth and final movement and state of *kriyā śakti*, represented by the letter "au", the energy of action becomes *sphuṭatama*, most vivid. So the energy of action has four states as represented in the letters "e, ai, o, au". And in these four states, the energy of action begins as not vivid *(asphuṭa kriyā śakti)*, then becomes vivid *(sphuṭa kriyā śakti)*, then more vivid *(sphuṭatara kriyā śakti)*, and finally most vivid *(sphuṭatama kriyā śakti)*. In this energy of action the reflection of the whole universe takes place. Although this universe is reflected in His total energy of action, yet this reflection has taken place primarily in His fourth energy of action which is represented by the letter "au".

The fact is, however, that even though this whole universe has been created, the nature of His Self, which is full of consciousness and bliss, has not been lessened at all. Nothing has happened. He is only residing in His own point. This state of Lord Śiva is represented by the letter "ṁ" *(anusvāra)*. The letter "ṁ", therefore, shows you that the existence of Lord Śiva has not moved from His own nature even though this whole universe is created in His Self.

The reflection of the universe, which has been explained earlier as being in the form of a cup shaped mirror, is represented by the sixteenth letter of the Sanskrit alphabet, *visarga*, the letter "ḥ". In *devanāgari* script the letter "ḥ" takes the form of the two points of the colon ":". And these two points of the *visarga* (:), represent the two cups in which the reflection of the universe takes place. These two points are known as *śiva bindu* and *śakti bindu*.

I have explained that the Sanskrit vowels, from the letter "a", which is *anuttara*, to the letter "ḥ", which is *visarga*, are *śiva tattva*. The remainder of the alphabet is *śakti tattva*, the universe of thirty five *tattvas*. And this universe is the reflection of His *svātantrya*. It is not created, it is a reflection. You may ask, if they are not created then how is each succeeding letter produced? Are they produced just by reflecting against the letter or are they produced from within their own self? They are not produced in either of these ways. Actually, it is the reflection of *svātantrya* that gives rise to each succeeding letter. In *cit śakti, ānanda śakti, icchā śakti, jñāna śakti,* and *kriyā śakti* the *svātantrya* of Lord Śiva is reflected. All of the elements *(tattvas)* are a reflection of the five energies of Lord Śiva. No element escapes from these five energies. Everything comes out from these five energies. It is His *svātantrya* that from these five energies first comes the five *mahābhūtas*, and then comes the five *tanmātras*, and then comes the five *karmendriyas*, and so on. And in each of these energies all of the five energies are existing. For example in *cit śakti* all the five energies, *cit śakti, ānanda śakti, icchā śakti, jñāna śakti,* and *kriyā śakti,* are present. At the same time you should understand that although in one energy all the energies are present yet only one energy is predominant. So five energies into five energies is twenty five and these are the first twenty five *tattvas*, from *prithvī* to *puruṣa*.

The five *mahābhūtas*, which are the five consonants from "ṅa" to "ka", are produced by *cit śakti (anuttara)* and *ānanda śakti*, which are one and which are the letters "a" and "ā", when mixed with His five energies. That reflection where His *cit śakti* is predominant is *ākāśa* (ether) and this is the letter "ṅa".[1] The reflection of His *ānanda śakti* is *vāyu* (air) and this is the letter "gha". The reflection of His *icchā śakti* is *agni* (fire) and this is the letter "ga". The reflection of His *jñāna śakti* is *jala* (water) and this is the letter "kha". And the reflection of His *kriyā śakti* is *prithvī* (earth) and this is the letter "ka".

---

1 *Śakti tattva* is a reflection of *Śiva tattva*. The reflective flow, therefore, is in each case from the last letter to the first letter, e.g., from (ṅa) to (ka), and the order of the consonants is reversed.

The five *tanmātras*, which are the consonants from "ña" to "ca", are produced by *icchā śakti*, the letters "i" and "ī", when it is mixed with the five energies. That reflection where His *cit śakti* is predominant is *śabda*, the residence of sound, and this is the letter "ña". The reflection of His *ānanda śakti* is *sparśa*, the residence of touch, and this is the letter "jha". The reflection of His *icchā śakti* is *rūpa*, the residence of form, and this is the letter "ja". The reflection of His *jñāna śakti* is *rasa*, the residence of taste, and this is the letter "cha". And the reflection of His *kriyā śakti* is *gandha*, the residence of smell, and this is the letter "ca".

The five *karmendriyas*, which are the five consonants from "na" to "ta" are produced by the letters "ṛi" and "ṝī", which is *anaśritaśiva*, in conjunction with the five energies. The five *jñānendriyas*, which are the five consonants from "na" to "ta", are produced by the same *tattva* through the letters "ḷi" and "ḹ".

The five *karmendriyas* are reflected as follows. The reflection where His *cit śakti* is predominant is *vāk*, the organ of speech, and this is the letter "na". The reflection of His *ānanda śakti* is *pāṇi*, the organ or action, and this is the letter "dha". The reflection of His *icchā śakti* is *pāda*, the organ of locomotion, and this is the letter "da". The reflection of His *jñāna śakti* is *pāyu*, the organ of excretion, and this is the letter "tha". And the reflection of His *kriyā śakti* is *upastha*, the active organ of sex, and this is the letter "ta".

The five *Jñānendriyas* are reflected in the following manner. The reflection where His *cit śakti* is predominant is *śrotra*, the cognitive organ of smell, and this is the letter "na". The reflection of His *ānanda śakti* is *tvak*, the cognitive organ of taste, and this is the letter "dha". The reflection of His *icchā śakti* is *cakṣu*, the cognitive organ of touch, and this is the letter "da". The reflection of His *jñāna śakti* is *rasanā*, the cognitive organ of sight, and this is the letter "tha". And the reflection of His *kriyā śakti* is *ghrāṇa*, the cognitive organ of hearing, and this is the letter "ta".

Jñāna śakti, which is the letters "u" and "ū", when mixed with the five energies produces the five elements *manas, buddhi, ahaṁkāra, prakṛti*, and *puruṣa*, which are the five consonants from "ma" to "pa". That reflection where His *cit śakti* is predominant is *puruṣa*, the limited self, and this is the letter "ma". The reflection of His *ānanda śakti* is *prakṛti*, nature, and this is the letter "bha". The reflection of His *icchā śakti* is *ahaṁkāra*, egoity, and this is the letter "ba". The reflection of His *jñāna śakti* is *buddhi*, intellect, and this is the letter "pha". And the reflection of His *kriyā śakti* is *manas*, mind, and this is the letter "pa".

The six internal states of *puruṣa*, which are *māyā, niyati, kāla, rāga, vidyā*, and *kalā*, are reduced to four by combining *niyati* with *rāga* and *kāla* with *kalā*. The four limitations which result from these combinations correspond to the next four semi-vowels. The limitations *kāla* and *kalā*, which are the limitations of time and creativity, correspond to the letter "ya". *Vidyā*, limited knowledge, corresponds to the letter "ra", *rāga* and *niyati*, the limitations of attachment and space, to "la", and *māyā*, the element of self ignorance and objectivity, corresponds to "va".

It cannot be said that these limitations are created by the energies of Lord Śiva as they represent the state of *puruṣa* internally. These limitations, therefore, are called *antaḥstha* because they reside inside *puruṣa*, one's own limited self. They are the internal state of limited *puruṣa*.

The four *tattvas, śuddhavidyā, īśvara, sadāśiva*, and *śakti*, are also not created by the energies of Lord Śiva. Instead, they are the swelling of the heat of His own nature. *Śuddhavidyā*, which is the state of *aham-aham /idam-idam*, is the letter "śa". *īśvara*, which is the state of *idam-aham*, is the letter "ṣa". *Sadāśiva*, which is the state of *aham-idam*, is the letter "sa".

Śakti, which is the state of *aham,* is the letter "ha". This is the reason that these four letters in grammar are called *ūṣma,* which means "the heat of His own nature." They are the expansion of the state of unlimited Being and as such are attached to the unlimited state of *puruṣa* which is the expansion of that state of unlimited Being.

The great Sanskrit grammarian Pāṇini also explains the alphabet as we do in our Śaivism.

akuhavisarjanīyānāṁ kaṇṭhaḥ l

The place where the following letters are produced is the throat.

a,   ā,   ka,   kha, ga,   gha,   ṅa,   ha,   ha

icuyaśānāṁ tālu l

The place where the following letters are produced is the palate.

i,   ī,   ca,   cha,   ja,   jha,   ña,   ya,   śa

ṛiturasānāṁ mūrdhā l

The place where the following letters are produced is the head.

ṛi,   r̄i,   ṭa,   ṭha, ḍa,   ḍha,   ṇa,   ra,   ṣa

litulasānāṁ dantāḥ l

The place where the following letters are produced is the teeth.

li,   lī,   ta,   tha,   da,   dha,   na,   la,   sa

upūpadhmānīyānāmoṣṭhau l

The place where the following letters are produced is the lips.

u,   ū,   pa,   pha,   ba,   bha,   ma,   upadhmānīya[2]

---

2. *upadhmānīya* is used in the recitation of *mantras* in the Vedas.

ñamananananānām nāsikā ca l

The place where the following letters are produced is the nose.

ña,   ma,   ṅa,   ṇa,   na

edaitoḥ kaṇṭhatālu l

The following letters are produced by the throat and palate.

e,   ai

odautoḥ kaṇṭhoṣṭam l

The following letters are produced by the throat and lips.

o,   au

vakārasya dantoṣṭham l

The following letter is produced by the teeth and lips.

va

jihvāmūlīyasya jihvāmūlam l

From the root of the tongue is produced.

jihvāmūlīya

nāsikānusvārasya l

From the nose is produced.

ṁ - anusvāra

The aim of *mātṛikācakra* is to function with the first and the last letter in either the way of Śiva or in the way of Śakti. To function in the way of Śiva take the first letter "a" which is the first step of Lord Śiva in the creative field, and combine this first letter with the last state of Lord Śiva, the letter "ha", which is the resting place and the last letter of *mātṛikācakra*. This also corresponds to Pāṇini's concept of *pratyāhāra*. Take the first letter along with the last letter and you will find that all of the letters are existing therein. The whole universe of letters will come in those two letters.

According to the rules of Sanskrit grammar we then, after combining the letters "a" and "ha", have to put the letter "ṁ" on the end and this creates the mantra of Lord Śiva, the mantra *aham*.[3] The letter "ṁ" has a special significance. It indicates that this whole *pratyāhāra*, which is contained in the letters from "a" to "ha", and which has produced the one hundred and eighteen worlds, the thirty six elements, and the five circles *(kalās)*, has in reality created nothing. It is just one point. This is the significance of the letter "ṁ", which is *anusvāra*.

The way of Śakti is the way of energy. The difference between Śakti *pratyāhāra* and Śiva *pratyāhāra* is that in Śakti *pratyāhāra* two Śaktis combine together and create a world of their own. Śakti is actually the existence of created Being. Śiva is the creator. Here Śakti wants to become independent of Śiva. To do so She must create a world of Her own. It is like what happens with bees. When the queen bee stops creating eggs then the worker, without mating, bees create eggs of their own. This is the mating of Śaktis. Śiva is put aside and Śakti combines with Śakti to create their own world which is the expansion of Śaktis. And this creation takes the first letter of the consonants, the letter "k", which is the first letter of the Śaktis and combines it with the last letter of the Śaktis, the last consonant, the letter "sa"[4] and produces the mantra of Śakti, the mantra "kṣa".

In the kingdom of *mātṛikācakra* there exists three kinds of *visargas*, three kinds of flow. These three *visargas* are known respectively as *śāmbhava visarga*, *śākta visarga*, and *āṇava visarga*.

The first *visarga* exists at the stage of *ānanda śakti*, and is

---

3. *Aham* is the *mantra* of Universal "I".

4. The letter "ha" is not part of this creation of the Śaktis because "ha" is a letter which is attached to Śiva and, therefore, does not recognize Her nature without Śiva. The letter "ha" is *apara visarga*, the gross *visarga* of Lord Śiva.

represented by the letter "ā". This *visarga* is known as *śām-bhava visarga*. The mode of this *visarga* is said to be *citta-pralayaḥ*. The word "*cittapralayaḥ*" indicates that state where your mind does not function, where only thoughtlessness exists. Here the mind does not work at all. This is a thought-less flow. This *śāmbhava visarga* is also known as *paravisar-ga*, the supreme *visarga*. This supreme *visarga* is concerned with Śiva.

The second *visarga* is known as *śākta visarga*. It is also known as *parapara visarga*, the highest cum lowest...medium *visarga*. This *visarga* is represented by the last letter of the vowels, which is also called *visargaḥ*, the letter "ḥ". The mode of this *visarga* is called *cittasambodhaḥ*. *Cittasambodhaḥ* indi-cates that state where awareness is maintained in one-pointed-ness.

The third and last *visarga* is called *āṇava visarga*. It is also known as *aparavisargaḥ*, the lower or inferior *visarga*. It is the *visarga* of the individual *(naraḥ)*. This *visarga* is attributed to the letter "ha", the last letter of the Sanskrit alphabet. The mode of this *visarga* is called *cittaviśrāntiḥ*. The word *cittaviśrāntiḥ* indicates that state where the mind rests in con-centration, where the mind takes a permanent seat in concen-tration.

Chapter Four

The Theory of Reflection
Pratibimbavādaḥ

In the ordinary worldly course sound is reflected outwardly in ether and inwardly in the ear. Touch is reflected outwardly in air and inwardly in the skin. Form is reflected outwardly in fire and in a mirror and inwardly in the eye. Taste is reflected outwardly in water and inwardly in the tongue. Smell is reflected outwardly in the earth and inwardly in the nose. These reflections, however, are just like the reflection in a mirror. They only take place individually. All five reflections are not available at once, only one thing is reflected in each. In a mirror form is reflected. Touch can not be reflected in a mirror nor can taste, smell, or sound. A mirror will only reflect form. It is only in Supreme God Consciousness that you find all five reflected at once. In fact, although these reflections are experienced individually in all of the organs, sight in the eye, sound in the ear, etc., these reflections could not even be observed if consciousness were not there. Awareness is needed and this is found in consciousness and not in the organs.

The universe, therefore, is reflected in the mirror of consciousness, not in the organs nor in the five gross elements. These are merely *tattvas* and can not reflect anything. The real reflector is consciousness. In consciousness, however, you see only the reflected thing and not anything that is reflected. That which is reflected *(bimba)* is in fact *svātantrya*. This whole universe is the reflection in God Consciousness of *svātantrya*.[1] There is no additional class of similar objects existing outside of this world that He reflects in His nature. The outside element, that which is reflected, is only *svātantrya*. The infinite variety which is created is only the expansion of *svātantrya*.[2]

You can understand this by taking the example of cause and effect. When a potter makes a pot he takes clay and gives form to that clay with his potters instruments such as a stick, string, and potters wheel. Within the potter's creative activity two kinds of causes can be distinguished. There is the material cause which in Sanskrit is called *upādāna kāraṇa*. This is that cause that travels with the effect. It cannot and does not become separated from the effect. Secondly, there is the formal cause which in Sanskrit is called *nimittakāraṇa*. The formal cause does not travel with the effect. The material cause is the potter's clay and the formal cause is the potter himself and his stick, string, and wheel. In the ordinary worldly course the reflected object *(bimba)* seems to be the cause of the reflection *(pratibimba)* because the reflected object cannot exist without that which is reflected. We have seen, however, that all reflection is really a reflection in God Consciousness. If the reflected object is really the cause of the reflection then what kind of cause is it? Is it the material cause, which travels with the

---

1. *Svātantrya śakta* is one with God Consciousness. There are not two elements such as the mirror and the object which is reflected in the mirror. The reflected and the reflection are one. The mirror, which is the absolutely independent will of God *(svātantrya)*, is God Consciousness.

2. yadvāpi kāraṇam kiñcit bimbatvena...

Tantrāloka: III;50

effect, or is it the formal cause, which does not travel with the effect? It cannot be the material cause because that would mean that there is something outside of God Consciousness which travels to become part of the effect which is the reflection. Yet, it is our theory in Śaivism that nothing can exist outside of God Consciousness. There cannot, therefore, be any agency which is separate from God Consciousness and which travels with the cause because if it is separate from God Consciousness and therefore from the effect it would not exist. If the reflection of some object is existing in the mirror of God Consciousness then of what is that object a reflection? We have seen that if the object which is reflected were to remain outside of God Consciousness then it would not exist. There is nothing, therefore, which is outside to be reflected in the mirror of God Consciousness. There is only the mirror. There is no external cause which has gone into the reflection which is the effect. There is only the mirror of God Consciousness.

But what then is the cause of this reflection? It is *svātantrya*, the absolutely independent will of God. *Svātantrya* is the mirror. It is the cause of this effect the reflection. Unlike ordinary reflection which we experience in the world wherein an object can be distinguished which is the cause of that reflection, in God Consciousness only the reflection exists and not anything that is separate and reflected *(bimba)*. In this causality the effect of which is the reflection, *svātantrya* is the formal cause *(nimittakāraṇa)* not the material cause *(upādānakāraṇa)*. It does not travel from the cause into the effect because, as I have explained, there is no cause which could be separate from God Consciousness. It is His free will that He wills and what He wills appears in the mirror of His Consciousness. It is simply His will *(svātantrya)*. In reality only the reflection exists and not anything that is reflected.

This universe, therefore, is found in the reflector of God Consciousness, not through the agency of anything of which it is a reflection *(bimba)* but through His *svātantrya* where the universe is contained in a seed form. *Svātantrya* is the seed of everything. Everything exists in the mirror of God Consciousness with *svātantrya* as its cause.

The theory of reflection *(pratibimbavāda)* is meant for advanced yogins. This theory teaches them how to be aware in their daily activities, while talking, while walking, while tasting, while touching, while hearing, while smelling. While they are doing all of these various actions they see that all of these actions move in their Supreme Consciousness. Their vision, their perception, heretofore limited becomes unlimited. The mode of their actions becomes absolutely unique. They see each and every action in their God Consciousness. They exist in the state of *sadāśiva*. Each and every action of their life becomes glorious. This is the awareness that comes from the practice of *pratibimba*.

Chapter Five

The Explanation of the Means
Upāyas

The meaning of the Sanskrit word *upāya* is 'means'. The word *upāya* in our Kashmir Śaivism is used to indicate the way and the means to enter from individual consciousness into Universal God Consciousness. Our Śaivism proclaims that there are three means for entering into Universal God Consciousness, *Śāmbhavopāya*, the supreme means, *śāktopāya*, the medium means, and *āṇavopāya*, the inferior means.

Śāmbhavopāya

Śāmbhavopāya, the supreme means, functions in *mātṛikā-cakra, pratyāhāra,* and *pratibimbavāda.* The definition given in the "Mālinīvijayottaratantram" for *Śāmbhavopāya* is, "The one who preserves thoughtlessness." By preserving thoughtlessness, that is, not having thoughts and maintaining the continuity of that thoughtlessness, and by the grace of the Master, he enters into that transcendental consciousness where he finds that this whole universe has come out from sentences and sentences from words and words from letters and letters from that real "I" which is *Parama Śiva*. Here he finds that this whole universe is reflected in his own consciousness and that it is reflected from within rather than from without.[1]

Śāmbhavopāya is called *icchopāya* because it originates from *icchā śakti* and because it is that means which exists in the state of the meant. In *Śāmbhavopāya* there are no means to travel upon. It is the meant. There is no where to go. You must reside only in the meant. The rest is automatic. Here, only the grace of your Master is necessary. It must be realized, however, that you yourself must come to this point where you reside in the meant and this you do by maintaining the continuity of thoughtlessness. Up to this point, therefore, there is still something to be done. When you reside only in the meant it is then the grace of your Master that carries you. You must reach that state where only your Master shines for you. This means that you must merge in your Masters consciousness. In this state you do not exist, only your Master exists. Masters select disciples for this *upāya* who are highly developed in awareness. Until then they will not be accepted by their Master for this *upāya*. In this *upāya* the Master functions more than does the disciple.

In our Kashmir Śaivism we say,

> svamuktimātre kasyāpi
> yāvadviśvavimocane I
> pratibodeti khadyota-
> ratnatārendu sūryavat II

Tantraloka: XIII:159

---

1. Akimciccintakasyaiva gurunā pratibodhatah I
   jāyate yah samāveśah śāmbhavo 'sāvudīritah I I

   Mālinīvijayottaratantram; II; V23

"A light bug shines only for himself, jewels
shine not only for themselves but for a few
others also, the stars shine for even more, the
moon shines for still more, and the sun shines
for the whole universe. In the same way he
who is established in the *sāmbhavopāya* state
shines like the midday sun for the whole universe."

As the light bug has sufficient light to show his own body
there are those yogins that are sufficient only for themselves,
they can not help anybody. There are also yogins, who like
jewels, shine so that their light illumines those that are near.
Those yogins that shine like stars illumine even more with
their light. Those that shine like the moon illumine still more.
But the Śaivaite yogī, established in *sāmbhavopāya*, is just like
the sun, he illumines the whole universe.

Śāktopāya

Śāktopāya is that *upāya* which is functioned by the means
of energies. *Śāktopāya* is called *jñānopāya* as it is the means
which originates from *jñāna śakti*, the energy of knowledge.
Here, the aspirant is more important than the Master because
he must make himself capable of receiving the Master's grace.
He must work to develop great velocity of awareness until he
reaches the "feet of the Master." By feet I do not mean the
physical feet of the Master. "Being at the feet of the Master"
means reaching that state where the aspirant is capable of
receiving the grace of the Master. Those that reach that state
are said to be at the "feet of the Master."

In *śāktopāya*, the yogi does not have to recite mantras or be
aware using his breath or concentrate on any particular spot.
He has only to see and concentrate on that Supreme Being that

is found in two actions without actions. This is called centering in the "Vijñāna Bhairava Tantra".[2]

In *śāktopāya* centering can be practiced between any and all actions and or thoughts. In centering, the yogī must develop great velocity of awareness. Great velocity means firmness of awareness. Awareness must not become loose. If the yogi's awareness becomes loose he will be forced out of *śāktopāya* into the lowest *upāya, āṇavopāya*. He will loose the right to tread on the path of *śāktopāya*. In his practice there must be continuity in the cycle of his awareness. Only by maintaining an unbroken chain of awareness will he be able to find out the reality between any two thoughts or actions. The practice of centering is meant to be functioned between any two actions or any two thoughts. He can center between any two thoughts or any two movements, between one thought and another thought, between waking and dreaming, between one step and the next step, between one breath and the next breath. All actions and all thoughts are the proper framework for the practice of *śāktopāya*. The *śāktopāya* yogī must simply insert breakless awareness in the center of any two actions or thoughts. If his awareness is faulty and is not breakless then he falls and enters into the lowest *upāya, āṇavopāya*.

Āṇavopāya

Āṇavopāya is concerned with *aṇu*, the individual soul. *Āṇavopāya* is that *upāya*, that means, which is functioned by the process of concentrating on *uccāra* (breathing), *karaṇa* (organs of sensation), *dhyāna* (contemplation), and *sthāna prakalpanā* (concentrating on some particular place).

---

2. "madhyaṁ samāśrayet"

Vijñāna Bhairava Tantra; Verse 61

The word 'uccāra' means 'breathing'. Uccāra actually means concentration on the breath. Concentration on the breath is the essential element of the practice of cakrodaya. In practicing cakrodaya you have to continue breathing deeply and find out the point, the centre between the two breaths, the incoming breath and the outgoing breath. This is the ending point, the beginning point, and also the centre of the span of the breath. In cakrodaya, however, the beginning points and ending points of the span of the breath are predominant. This is uccāra, concentration on the breath. It can be either with sound or without sound.

'Karana' means 'organ' and in particular it means 'sense organ'. Concentrating on karana means having and maintaining onepointedness through vision or through any other sense organ. In karana the sense of sight and seeing is predominant. For example, in concentrating on karana through the sense of sight you have to look at some particular thing. You must go on looking without blinking your eyes. You should go on seeing that one point with unbroken awareness. And when that point vanishes, and it should and will vanish when you enter in that vastness of the centre, that is the end. If you were to practice concentrating on karana through the sense of hearing then you have to listen to some sound and continue listening and repeating that sound again and again and hearing that sound. You can also practice by concentrating on some taste or some particular sensation of touch. In karana you can employ all the five organs of sensation, however, with those senses other than sight you have to remain aware of where the first sensation arises. This is the way of karana in āṇavopāya and in the long run this creates onepointedness.

The word 'dhyāna' means contemplation. It is another mode in āṇavopāya. Dhyāna is contemplation on some point. There are different forms of dhyāna. For example, you are practicing dhyāna when you contemplate on the lotus in your heart, or on the meaning of some *mantra*[3] such as the *mantra* "*so'ham*" or the *mantra* "*śiva*". This is a higher form of *āṇavopāya* because it is contemplation without any shape, without any form. If you were to contemplate on Lord Śiva as having a particular form, a particular shape, that is a lower form of *āṇavopāya*, it is contemplation with form.

Therefore, anytime in meditation that you have *mantra* then you have *dhyāna*. And along with *dhyāna* you can also adjust *karaṇa* and *uccāra*, but not in the beginning.

'*Sthāna prakalpanā*' means concentration on some particular place. The higher form of *sthāna prakalpanā*, which is a practice in higher *āṇavopāya*, is that practice where you have to find out where each aspect of reality is found in the span of the breath. You have to see where the *devas* are residing, where the *lokapālas* are residing, where is the location of dawn, where is the location of morning, where is the location of midday, where is the location of sunset *(sandhyā)*, where is the location of midnight, where is that location which is the time when the sun moves toward the Northern side, and where is that location which is the time when the sun moves to the Southern side. These are all *sthāna prakalpanā*, and these are the particular points you have to concentrate on, to discover in the course of your breath.[4] The practice of *sthāna prakalpanā* is simply to see the vastness of this universe in one breath.

The second and lower form of *sthāna prakalpanā*, which is a practice in lower *āṇavopāya*, is where you concentrate on

---

3. All *mantras* have meaning.

4. In the practice of *sthāna prakalpanā* there are points in the breath which you must concentrate on. In the practice of *uccāra* there is no need to concentrate on each and every point in passage of the breath. In this practice you have to concentrate on only one point.

different points in the body. These particular places for concentration are divided into three. One particular place for concentration is between the two eyebrows *(bhrūmadhya)*. The
second place for concentration is the pit of the throat *(kaṇtha
kūpa)*. And the third place of concentration is the heart
(hṛidaya).

All of these processes, *uccāra, karaṇa, dhyāna,* and *sthāna
prakalpanā*, are called the *upāyas* of *jīva*, the means of the
individual, and are the means which exist in *āṇavopāya*.

Āṇavopāya is the means found in the world of duality and is
known as *bhedopāya*. The means which exists in the world of
mono-duality, in the world where duality and non-duality exist
together, is *śāktopāya* and is called *bhedābhedopāya*. That
means which exists in the world of pure monism *(abheda)* is
śāmbhavopāya and is called *abhedopāya*.

Śāmbhavopāya is also called *icchopāya* as it is the means
which exists in *icchā śakti*. The means which exists in *jñāna
śakti* is *śāktopāya* and is called *jñānopāya*. *Āṇavopāya* is
called *kriyopāya* because it is the means which is found in
kriyā śakti.

The difference between *āṇavopāya, śāktopāya,* and
śāmbhavopāya is this. In *āṇavopāya* the strength of your
awareness is such that you have to take the support of everything as an aid to maintaining and strengthening your awareness. Though you concentrate on the center you need to take
the support of two things for concentrating on that center. In
śāktopāya your awareness is strengthened to the extent that
only one point is needed as a support for your concentration
and that point is the center. In *śāktopāya* you begin with the
center and then become established in that center. In
śāmbhavopāya the strength of your awareness is such that no
support is needed. You are already residing in the meant.
There is no where to go, just reside at your own point. The rest
is automatic.

It is important to realize that though there are different *upāyas*, yet all of these *upāyas* lead you to the state of one transcendental consciousness. The difference in these *upāyas* is that *āṇavopāya* will carry you in a long way, *śāktopāya* in a shorter way, and *śāmbhavopāya* in the shortest way. Although the ways are different, the point to be achieved is one.

Anupāya

Beyond these three *upāyas*, *śāmbhavopāya*, *śāktopāya*, and *āṇavopāya*, there is another *upāya*. Although it is not actually an *upāya*, yet it is mentioned in Kashmir Śaivism. This *upāya* is called *anupāya*. The word '*anupāya*' means 'no *upāya*'. 'Thoughtlessness' is called *śāmbhavopāya*. 'Onepointedness' is called *śāktopāya*. 'Concentration on and with the support of *mantra* and breathing and all other elements' is called *āṇavopāya*. Above all of these is *anupāya*. in *anupāya* the aspirant has only to observe that nothing is to be done. Be as you are. If you are talking, go on talking. If you are sitting, go on sitting. Do not do anything, only reside in your being. This is the nature of *anupāya*. *Anupāya* is attributed to *ānanda śakti* of *Śiva* and is called *ānandopāya*.

Chapter Six

The Theory of Speech
Vāk

When the aspirant resides in the *śāmbhava* state, in complete universal Iness *(pūrṇāhantā)*, he is travelling in the kingdom of *vāk*, "speech". Here he resides in the principal and supreme speech which is called *parāvāk*. And not only does this aspirant reside in that state of *parāvāk*, but he travels in other sounds also. He comes out and he goes in. He has the ability of travelling from the supreme to the gross and from the gross to the supreme. He can ascend and descend without varying his consciousness. His consciousness will remain the same in each and every state.

The word *"parā"* means "supreme", and *parā vāk* is the supreme speech. It is that soundless sound which resides in your own universal consciousness. It is the supreme sound which has no sound. It is the life of the other three kinds of speech which comprise the kingdom of speech, *paśyantī*, *madhyamā*, and *vaikharī*, and yet it does not come in this kingdom of speech. The aspirants purpose in the kingdom of speech is to travel from *paśyantī* to *madhyamā* and then to *vaikharī*. In your journey you do not travel to *parā* because *parā* is supreme.

Paśyantī vāk is that speech which is without differentiation *(nirvikalpa)*. Take for example the perception of some object such as a watch. When you look at this watch you feel that it is a watch. But do not go that far in your perceiving, you have to see something more, what you saw before you felt that it was a watch. Before that you observed something white, not a watch, only something white. This is that state which is partially undifferentiated *(nirvikalpa)* and partially differentiated *(vikalpa)*. This is moving to the first flow of the perception of that which you are observing. At this point in your perception you see only a white shade. Go still further forward in your perception. You will only see that there is some sensation of seeing. You will not see anything. This is *paśyantī vāk*. In this first flow of your perceiving, you were observing, you were looking. but you were not seeing anything. It is only afterwards that you saw a watch. This kind of observation, which takes place at the level of *paśyantī vāk*, is in the *nirvikalpa* state.

Paśyantī vāk is that state where a person is experiencing, observing the world, but not seeing anything. It is only pure sensation without any differentiation *(vikalpa)*, without any thought. In our Śaivaite literature the state of *paśyantī vāk* is described as "*śikharastha jñāna*". "*Śikharastha jñāna*" means knowing something while situated at the top. For example, when you climb to the top of a hill and see below a whole town. When you observe that town, you observe it in its entirety. You do not observe it as a collection of separate entities, one by one, such as this is a tree, this is a path, this is a motor car, these are people moving about. Rather, you generally see the town as a whole without differentiation, such as the perception 'this is the town of Srinagar', 'this is the city of London'. And this kind of perception where you perceive something, such as our example of the town, as a whole and not in distinct parts is called *śikharastha jñāna*. This is that seeing which is without thought. And in the same way you perceive and observe at the level of *paśyantī vāk*.[1]

The next state of speech *(vāk)* is called *madhyamā vāk*. *Madhyamā vāk* is between the lowest speech, *vaikharī*, and the highest speech, *paśyantī*. This is the reason that it is called *madhyamā*, it is speech in the middle state. *Madhyamā vāk* is that state of mind where you reside only in thoughts. This state is only mental. It is without words, sentences, or letters. When you are asleep and dreaming you are residing in *madhyamā vāk*. Here you are residing only in the mind, not in action and, therefore, you are devoid of sensation.

The third state of speech is called *vaikharī vāk*. The term "*vaikharī*" means "gross, rough". This gross speech is ordinary speech. When you utilize *vaikharī vāk* you have to use your tongue and lips.

These three states of speech are respectively called subtlest, subtle, and gross. Gross speech is *vaikharī vāk*, subtle speech is *madhyamā vāk*, and subtlest speech is *paśyantī vāk*. In considering each of these three states of speech, each state of speech is itself also gross *(sthūlā)*, subtle *(sūkṣmā)*, and subtlest *(parā)*. Therefore there is gross *paśyantī*, subtle *paśyantī*, and subtlest *paśyantī*, gross *madhyamā*, subtle *madhyamā*, and subtlest *madhyamā*, gross *vaikharī*, subtle *vaikharī*, and subtlest *vaikharī*. In Śaivism the location of these different refine-

---

1. A baby experiences in the *nirvikalpa* state, without thought. As the baby grows up his experiences are both *nirvikalpa* and *savikalpa*. When he becomes old he only experiences in the *savikalpa* state. Here, in this state of differentiation, he is only barking, "do this, do this, do this". Yet, there is no strength in doing this. In the end this is a degraded state for individual souls. He has lost the charm of that supremeness. To regain that supremeness you have to gain the *nirvikalpa* state in this *savikalpa* state. It is only then that the *nirvikalpa* state will remain permanently.

ments of sound are indicated for the easy apprehension of the aspirant.

First, I will explain to you gross *(sthūlā) paśyantī*, then gross *madhyamā*, and then gross *vaikharī*. Next, I will explain subtle *(sūkṣmā) paśyantī*, subtle *madhyamā*, and subtle *vaikharī*. And finally, I will explain subtlest *(parā) paśyantī*, subtlest *madhyamā*, and subtlest *vaikharī*.

When you play on any metal strung instrument, such as a sitāra, the sound which is produced by that metal strung instrument resides in gross *paśyantī*. And when one concentrates on that sound which exists in gross *paśyantī* they should enter in *samādhi*, enter in that supreme transcendental Being. In fact, it is said in our Kashmir Śaivism that those who can not enter into their real nature while listening to this sound of the metal strung instrument are worthless. They have no capacity, no ability of concentration. That sound should and must take you inside because that sound is *paśyantī*, even though it is gross *paśyantī*. The sound of gross *madhyamā* is produced by that drum instrument which is covered by leather. Concentration on this gross *madhyamā* is also helpful for carrying the aspirant inside his own real nature.[2]

The third speech, gross *vaikharī* is said to be all the sounds which are produced by the mouth, through the contact of the lips and tongue. In this state of speech no concentration is possible. No one can enter into *samādhi* by concentrating on this gross *vaikharī* except for that aspirant who is residing in the *śāmbhava* state. He enters into *samādhi* through ordinary talk.

_____

2. Although it is easier to enter into gross *paśyantī* than it is to enter into gross *madhyamā*, it is more difficult to reside in gross *paśyantī* than it is to reside in gross *madhyamā*. You can not easily reside in gross *paśyantī* unless you have the grace of the Master.

This, therefore, also leads him to that supreme consciousness.

To explain subtle *(sūksmā) paśyantī*, subtle *madhyamā*, and subtle *vaikharī*, I will combine them and explain them together as is traditionally done in our Śaivism.[3] The inclination in thought that *(sadajam karomi)* "I will play this string instrument", or the inclination *(madhuram vādayāmi)* "I will play on this drum", or the inclination *(bruve vacah)* "I will speak to you", is subtle. It is this thought which resides in the mind, in the consciousness, of that person. And this is not so much a thought as an inclination to think this thought. It is that point, that inclination, that first comes in his mind. In these three inclinations to think a thought, the inclination *(sadajam karomi)* "I will play this string instrument" is subtle *paśyantī*, the inclination *(madhuram vādayāmi)* "I will play this drum" is subtle *madhyamā*, and the inclination *(bruve vacah)* "I will speak to you" is subtle *vaikharī*.

And when only the sensation of the thought *(sadajam karomi)* "I will play this string instrument", or *(madhuram vādayāmi)* "I will play this drum", or *(bruve vacah)* "I will speak to you", begins, when it just starts to take' rise, that sensation, which is only in the thoughtless world, is subtlest. It is before desire. And that sensation of the thought *(sadajam karomi)* "I will play this string instrument", is subtlest *paśyantī*. The sensation of the thought *(madhuram vādayāmi)* "I will play this drum" is subtlest *madhyamā*. And the sensation of the thought *(bruve vacah)* "I will speak to you" is subtlest *vaikharī*.

For those aspirants who reside in the *śāmbhava* state there are no restrictions of only traveling in some particular *vāk*. They can travel in each and every state of *vāk*, and yet remain in the *śāmbhava* state. The aspirant of the *śāmbhava* state can

---

3. Abhinavagupta explains these three states of subtle sound together in the third chapter of the *Tantrāloka*.

travel in gross *paśyantī*, subtle *paśyantī*, and subtlest *paśyantī*, gross *madhyamā*, subtle *madhyamā*, and subtlest *madhyamā*, gross *vaikharī*, subtle *vaikharī*, and subtlest *vaikharī*, and still remain in his transcendental state. This is the greatness of the *śāmbhava* state.

The aspirant of the *śākta* state, which is that aspirant who has gained transcendental consciousness through adopting the means of *śāktopāya*, for him there are only two movements of speech in which he can travel, subtle and subtlest. If he tries to travel in the movement of gross speech he will be scattered, he will go astray from his Reality.

Those aspirants who are in the state of *āṇavopāya*, can only utilize the gross movement of speech because they have no experience of the subtle or the subtlest states of speech. They must, therefore, initially practice on the gross state of speech. In the long run their concentration on that gross speech will finally carry them to *śāktopāya* where they will then reside in their own nature.

Chapter Seven

The Three Impurities
Malas

In our Śaiva system there are three *malas* or impurities. These *malas* reside in *māyā*. They do not reside in *svātantrya śakti*. Even though *svātantrya śakti* and *māyā* are one, yet they are different in the sense that *svātantrya śakti* is that state of energy which can produce the power of going down and coming up again, both at will, whereas *māyā* will only give you the strength of coming down and not the ability of rising up again. Once you have come down you can not move up again. This is the reality of the state of *māyā*. It binds you.

Māyā śakti is that universal energy which is owned by the individual being, the individual soul. And when that same universal energy is owned by the universal being it is called *svātantrya śakti*. *Svātantrya śakti* is pure universal energy. Impure universal energy is *māyā*. It is only the formation that changes through a difference of vision. When you experience *svātantrya śakti* in a crooked way it becomes *māyā śakti* for you. And when you realize that same *māyā śakti* in Reality then that *māyā śakti* becomes *svātantrya śakti* for you. Therefore, *svātantrya śakti* and *māyā śakti* are actually only one and the three impurities *(malas)*, which are to be explained here, reside in *māyā śakti* not in *svātantrya śakti*.

The three impurities *(malas)* are respectively gross *(sthūla)*, subtle *(sūkṣma)*, and subtlest *(para)*. The gross impurity is called *kārma-mala*. It is connected with actions. It is that impurity which inserts the impressions such as those which are expressed in the experiences, "I am happy, I am not well, I have pain, I am a great man, I am really a lucky man", in the consciousness of the individual being. This impurity of action *(kārmamala)*, is *śubhāśubhavāsanā*, the impressions of pleasure and pain. And these impressions of pleasure and pain actually remain in your individual consciousness.[1]

The next impurity is called *māyīya mala*. This impurity creates differentiation in one's own consciousness. It is the impurity of ignorance *(avidyā)*. It is the subtle impurity. The thoughts, "This house is mine, that house is not mine; This man is my friend, that man is my enemy; She is my wife, she is not my wife", are all created by *māyīya mala*. *māyīya mala* creates duality. *Māyīya mala* is *bhinnavedyaprathā*, the feeling that myself and others are different. Thus you feel that what you have is different from what others have, that some things are yours and other things are not yours. This is that impurity which makes Lord Śiva appear as many rather than as one.

The third impurity is called *āṇavamala*. It is the subtlest impurity. *Āṇavamala* is the particular internal impurity of the individual. Although he reaches the nearest state of the consciousness of Śiva, yet he has no ability to catch hold of that state of Śiva. That inability is the creation of *āṇavamala*. For

---

1. An aspirant who resides in the highest state, *anupāya*, or in the *śāmbhava* state would have no *malas*. If he were to hurt himself he would not feel pain in the way a bound and limited individual would. Instead he would feel a sensation of consciousness. And yet he would not be attached to that sensation. It would take him in, into his own Being.

example, if you are conscious of your own nature and yet that consciousness fades away and it fades away quickly, this fading is caused by *āṇavamala*.

Āṇavamala is *apūrṇatā*, non–fullness. It is the feeling of being incomplete. Due to this impurity you feel incomplete in every way. Because of this feeling you create *abhilāṣā*, the desire for completion. As you feel that you are not complete you desire to become complete. For example, if I have the desire for some particular thing then it means that I feel that I do not have this thing. This feeling, that you do not have this thing, is caused by *āṇavamala*.

Though you feel incomplete, knowing that there is some lack in you, yet you do not know what this lack really is. You want to hold everything, and yet no matter what you hold you do not fill your sense of lacking, your gap. You cannot fill this lacking unless the Master points it out to you and then carries you to that.

Of these three impurities, *āṇavamala* and *māyīya mala* are not in action, they are only in perception, in experience. It is *kārma mala* which is in action.

Chapter Eight

Seven States of the Seven Perceivers
Pramātrin

Seven states of the seven *pramātrins* (perceivers) and their importance. The first state is called *sakala*. The *sakala* state is that state where perception takes place in the objective world and not in the subjective world. In other words I would call this state the state of *prameya*, the state of the object of perception. This state is realized by its *pramātri* — the observer who resides in this state, in the field of objectivity and its world.

The second state is called *pralayākala*. This state is the state of negation, where the whole world is negated. And the one who resides in this world of negation is called *pralayākala pramātri*, the observer of the *pralayākala* state. And this *pramātri*, this perceiver, does not experience the state of this voidness because this state is actually the state of unawareness. This state would be, in other words, observed at the time of *mūrcchā*, when one becomes comatose, which is like unnatural and heavy sleep, like deep sleep which is void of dreams. And the observer, *pralayākala pramātri*, resides in that void unawareness.

These two states function in the state of individuality not in the state of your real nature. These are states of worldly people not spiritualists.

The third state is called *vijñānākala pramātri*. This state is experienced by those people who are on the path of yoga. In this state the yogī experiences at times awareness but this awareness is not active awareness and at other times his awareness is active but he is not aware of that active awareness.[1] This *vijñānākala pramātri*, therefore, takes place in two ways, sometimes it is full of action (*svātantrya*) without awareness and sometimes it is full of awareness without action.[2]

In the first state, the state of *sakala pramātri*, all the three *malas*, *āṇava*, *māyīya*, and *kārma mala*, are active. In the second state, the state of *pralayākala pramātri*, *kārma mala* is gone and only two *malas* remain, *āṇava mala* and *māyīya mala*. These two *malas* are concerned with thought rather than action whereas *kārma mala* is concerned with action. In the third state of *pramātrin*, the state of *vijñānākala pramātri*, only one *mala*, *āṇava mala*, remains while the other two *malas*, *māyīya mala* and *kārma mala*, have ceased functioning.

The fourth state of the observer is called *śuddhavidyā* and

---

1. svātantryāhānirbodhasya svātantrasyāpyabodhatā
   (dvidhāṇavam malamidam svasvarūpāpahānitaḥ)

   Īsvarapratyābhijñā Kārikā III;2:4

   "Āṇava mala is two fold. It is the cause of the ignorance of free will and it is also the cause of the loss of free will. Thus it carries one away from their own Real Self."

2. Being full of awareness is *jñānapūrṇa*, full of knowledge. Being full of action is *svātantrya*, full of absolute independence.

its observer is called *mantra*[3] *pramātṛi*. In this state the observer is always aware with *svātantṛya*. In this state of *mantra pramātṛi* all the *malas* have been removed and its observer observes only the state of his own Self, his own Real nature, full of consciousness, full of bliss, full of independent will, full of knowledge, and full of action. Hence this state, though it is not a stable state, is the real state of Śiva. And the *mantra* for this state is *ahaṁ ahaṁ, idaṁ idaṁ*. The meaning of the first section of this *mantra, ahaṁ ahaṁ*, is that in this state he experiences that he is the reality, the Real nature of Self, the Truth of this whole universe. On the other hand, the meaning of the second section of this *mantra, idaṁ idaṁ*, tells us that he also experiences that this universe is false, unreal. Because this state is not stable the yogī does not always remain in this state. The experience of this state comes and goes. Sometimes he experiences this state and sometimes he does not experience this state. Sometimes he experiences only *ahaṁ ahaṁ*. Sometimes, when his consciousness is a little damaged, he experiences only *idaṁ idaṁ*. Therefore, his reality of Self remains unstable and uncertain.

The next state is called *īśvara pramātṛi* and its observer is called *mantreśvara*. The word *mantreśvara* means the one who has sovereignty on *mantra (ahaṁ - I)*. This state is like the state of *mantra pramātṛi*, full of consciousness, full of bliss, full of will, full of knowledge, and full of action, however, this state is a more stable state. The aspirant finds more sta-

---

3. The meaning of the word mantra in the sense that it is being used here is found in the roots which comprise it, manana and trāṇa. Manana means awareness, possessing complete knowledge. Trāṇa means complete protection, protection from all the four sides, that protection which protects the whole ignorant world from ignorance. Therefore mantra is that knowledge by which we are protected.

bility in this state. The *mantra* for this state is *idaṁ ahaṁ*. The meaning of this *mantra* is that the aspirant feels in this state of *mantreśvara* that this whole universe is not false, on the contrary, he feels that this whole universe is the expansion of his own nature. In the state of *mantra pramātṁi* he felt that the universe was false, that he was the truth of this reality. Now he unites the state of the universe with the state of his own consciousness. This is actually the unification of *jīva*, the individual, with Śiva, the universal.

The next state is the state of *sadāśiva*. The observer of this state is called *mantra maheśvara*. In this state the observer finds himself to be absolutely one with the Universal Transcendental Being. He experiences this state to be more valid, more solid, and deserving of confidence. Once he enters into this state there is no question of falling from it at all. This is the established state of his Self, his own Real nature. The *mantra* of this state is *ahaṁ idaṁ*. The meaning of this *mantra* is, I am this universe. Here, in this state, he finds his Self in the universe while in the previous state of *mantreśvara* he found the universe in his Self. This is the difference. Here, he realizes his Self in the universe. In the former state he realized the universe in his Self.

The seventh and last state is the state of Śiva and the observer of this state is no other than Śiva Himself. In the other six states the state is one thing and the observer is something else. In this final state the state is Śiva and the observer is also Śiva. There is nothing outside Śiva. The *mantra* in this state is *ahaṁ*, universal I. Thisness is gone, melted in His Iness. This state is completely full with consciousness, bliss, will, knowledge, and action.

The reader must know that in these seven states of seven *pramātrins* there are seven *pramātri śaktis*. These are the energies of the seven *pramātrins*. The first energy is that energy by which one is capable of residing in all the three *malas* and thereby remaining in the state of *sakala* is called *sakala pramātṛi śakti*. The second energy is that energy which makes one capable of residing in unawareness, in voidness (*śūnya*). And this energy is called *pralayākala pramātṛi śakti*. That energy which enables one to be seated in the state of *vijñānākala*, where only *āṇava mala* is active, is called *v-ijñānākala pramātṛi śakti*. The fourth energy makes it possible for you to reside in the state of *ahaṁ ahaṁ, idaṁ idaṁ* in the state of *mantrapramātṛi*, which is the state of *śuddhavidyā*, is called *mantra pramātṛi śakti*. In this state all of the malas have vanished completely. The fifth energy is that energy which carries you in the state of *mantreśvara* and is called *montreśvara pramātṛi śakti*. This is the energy which is found in the state of *īśvara*. The sixth energy is that energy which sentences the yogī to the state of *sadāśiva*, the state of *mantra maheśvara*. This energy is called *mantra maheśvara śakti* and it carries the aspirant in the perception of *ahaṁ idaṁ* where he finds his Iness in the universe. The seventh energy is the state of that energy of Śiva. This energy strengthens His state which is already established in the state of Supreme Iness, the state of the universal and transcendental "I". This energy is called *Śiva pramātṛi śakti*.

It is for this reason that in the *Mālinī Vijaya Tantram* the purpose of these seven states is fully described for the benefit of the aspirant. This description is called *pañcadaśavidhiḥ*, the mode of fifteen fold thoughts for rising and coming back, for ascending and descending. This means that the theory of the seven *pramātrins* and their seven energies is meant not only for rising but also for descending. The aspirant must be capable of both rising and descending. The one who rises and cannot descend is incomplete. It is that aspirant who can rise and also descend simultaneously who is considered to be complete and full.

So in conclusion, the state of Śiva is actually that state where Śiva can rise and descend, and after descending He can again rise. On the other hand the state of individuality is that state where Śiva descends from the state of Śiva to the state of individuality and then having descended cannot rise again. This is the difference between the reality of Śiva and the reality of individual.

Chapter Nine

The Seven Processes of the Seven Perceivers

In considering the seven states of the seven *pramātṛins* it is important for you to know where these different states exist. The state of *sakala* is found to be existing from *pṛithvī tattva*, the element earth, to *puruṣa tattva*. That is, all of the *tattvas* existing from *pṛithvī tattva* up to and including *puruṣa tattva* are established in the *sakala pramātṛi* state. The *pralayākala* state is found to be existing in *māyā tattva*. *Māyā tattva* is simply voidness, a gap. Contained in *māyā tattva* are the two *malas*, *āṇava mala* and *māyīya mala*. In *māyā tattva kārma mala* is subsided existing at this point only in seed form. Therefore, in the state of *pralayākala* one *mala*, *kārma mala*, has become inactive and from the experiencer's point of view has disappeared. *Āṇava* and *māyīya mala*, however, remain and are active.

Between *māyā tattva* and *śuddhavidyā tattva* there is a large gap which has not come in the class of the *tattvas*. This semi *tattva* is called *mahāmāyā tattva* even though it is not actually a *tattva*. This *tattva* causes only dissolution, going down and down. In *mahāmāyā tattva* is found the existence of *v-ijñānākala*. In *śuddhavidyā tattva* you find the state of *mantra pramātā* which is also called *śuddhavidyā pramātṛi*. In *īśvara tattva* you find the state of *mantreśvara pramātṛi* which is also called *īśvara pramātā*. And in *sadāśiva tattva* you will experience the state of *mantra maheśvara pramātṛi*.

In the above six states you will find that both the state and the state holder, the state and the experiencer of that state, exist together simultaneously. Both shine at the same time in these six states. In the seventh state, however, the state of Śiva *pramātṛi*, neither the experiencer *(pramātṛi)* nor the object of experience *(prameya)*, the state and the state holder, are found separately. Here Śiva is the state and Śiva is also the state holder. The observer and the observed are one in the state of Śiva *pramātṛi*. Hence, all of the thirty six *tattvas* are found in the states of the seven *pramātṛins*.

The fifteen fold process teaches us how to rise from the lowest state of objectivity and get entry in subjective consciousness. This fifteen fold process is comprised of seven *pramātṛins*, seven *pramātṛi śaktis* (energies) and the fifteenth, the object. In this process we begin with objectivity in the state of *sakala pramātṛi*. For instance, take any form which is created with the element earth such as an earthen pot. Look at the pot, just go on looking at it, seeing it. The jug is the object that we are perceiving. This is objectivity in the state of *sakala pramātṛi*. At the time when you are perceiving the pot you forget the state of observer, the one who is observing this pot. At the time of perceiving the pot you yourself become the pot. You are completely unaware of your own consciousness. This is the state of *svarūpa*, the fifteenth, complete objectivity. Here the subjective state has merged in the objective state. This is the state of complete objectivity in the *sakala* state. This is the starting point in the fifteen fold process of rising. It is from here that you must begin by and by to develop your awareness. While perceiving the pot you develop awareness of the perceiver and there you will find the state of *sakala pramātṛi*. The means by which you peiceive this state of *sakala pramātṛi* is called *sakala pramātṛi śakti*, the energy of *sakala pramātṛi*.

Then, in continuing the fifteen fold process of rising, you must also rise from this state of *sakala pramātṛi* where you are fully aware of yourself as the perceiver. Here in this state the objective element, the pot, is gone and only you, the perceiver, remain. In this state of the perceiver, in order to continue to rise, you must now also remove the thought of the perceiver. This is due to the fact that along with the thought of being the perceiver, in the background the perceived also exists. When the perceiver exists the perceived is also to be found in the background, not vividly, but it is there. We must, therefore, also rise from the state of the perceiver. And while rising from the state of the perceiver to the state of the super perceiver you fall in voidness. This voidness is the state of *pralayākala*[1] *pramātṛi*. This *pralayākala* state is absolutely void.

When you are in the *pralayākala* state it is almost certain that you will lose consciousness. When you do not loose consciousness of your Being and you are in the *pralayākala* state then you are in the state of *vijñānākala pramātṛi*.

From the state of *vijñānākala pramātṛi* you are carried automatically to *mantrapramātṛi* and then to *mantreśvara pramātṛi* and then to *mantramaheśvara pramātṛi* and finally to the state of Śiva. You must apply effort only up to the crossing of *māyā*. *Māyā* is the border line. Once you have crossed *māyā*, which is the state of *pralayākala*, then everything is automatic, everything is solved[2]

---

1. The Sanskrit word kalā means 'sensation'. The Sanskrit word Sa-kala, therefore, means 'with sensation' and the Sanskrit word pralayākala means the 'dissolution' or 'absence' of sensation.

This is the reality of *pañcadaśīvidhiḥ*, the fifteen fold process of rising. This process can and must be functioned in each
and every field, the subjective field, the cognitive field, and
the objective field, from *prithvī tattva*, the element earth, to
puruṣa tattva. You can function this process only in *prithvī
tattva* and all the processes will be complete or you can function this process on the organs and all the processes will be
``complete. You can function this process on any of the *tattvas*
from *prithvī* to *puruṣa tattva*.

The next process which you must function is called
trayodaśavidhiḥ. The Sanskrit word *trayodaśavidhiḥ* means
'thirteen fold process'. The thirteen fold process includes six
pramātrins, six *pramātri* energies, and the object. This thirteen
fold process can only be functioned when you have mastered
the fifteen fold process. The object of this thirteen fold process
on which you have to function and from which you have to
rise is *sakala pramātri* including its energy. And the observer
in this process is *pralayākala* and the means by which it
observes *sakala pramātri* is *pralayākala śakti*. First you have
to rise from some being existing in no being. Then you will
travel. The perceiver must perceive the duality which is individual being in voidness without any thought. And when that
perception is no longer voidness then it will be all consciousness. This is the state of *vijñānākala pramātri*. From this state
you rise automatically to *mantra pramātri, mantreśvara
pramātri, mantra maheśvara pramātri*, and finally to *Śiva
pramātri*. This is the thirteen fold process as it is explained in

---

2. It is the Grace of God which carries you from the lowest point to the
   highest point. You are automatically carried after you cross the boundry
   of *māyā*, however, His Grace has been with you throughout the whole of
   your journey. His Grace is always there in the background for if it were
   not there you could not do anything.

the *Mālinī Vijaya Tantra*. This process is meant for highly qualified yogins.

The fifteen fold process and the thirteen fold process differ in that in the fifteen fold process you have to rise from objectivity to Universal Being whereas in the thirteen fold process you have nothing to do with the objective world. In the thirteen fold process you have to rise from individuality, from individual being, to Universal Being. In the fifteen fold process once you have attained the state of Universal Being the process is complete and you then have to step up to the thirteen fold process.

After you have completed the thirteen fold process then you must begin *ekādaśavidhih*, the eleven fold process. The eleven fold process includes five *pramātrins*, five *pramātṛi* energies and the object from which you have to rise. In this process the object is the state of *pralayākala pramātṛi*, complete and utter voidness. In this process then, you have to rise from voidness. When you have the capacity to rise from voidness you are greater. You must be very subtle to be able to rise from voidness. It is absolutely impossible for *sakala pramātṛi* to rise from voidness. It is easy to rise from objectivity, or from subtle things, but it is extremely difficult to rise from voidness.

Even though you have attained Universal Being in the fifteen fold process of rising you do not have the capacity to maintain that universal state. The purpose of functioning these increasingly difficult processes is to strengthen your capacity of rising so that you can maintain this capacity and never fall from the state of Universal Being.

When, in the eleven fold process, you make *pralayākala pramātṛi* the object and starting point of this process then the perceiver will be *vijñānākala pramātṛi*. He will automatically travel from *vijñānākala pramātṛi* to *mantra pramātṛi*, *mantreśvara pramātṛi*, *mantra maheśvara pramātṛi*, and finally to *Śiva pramātṛi*.

After completing the eleven fold process you must begin *navātmaviddhiḥ*, the nine fold process. This process includes four *pramātrins*, four *pramātri* energies, and the object. In this process *vijñānākala pramātri* is the object and the perceiver is *mantra pramātri*. From *mantra pramātri* rising will take place automatically and you will rise to *mantreśvara pramātri*, *mantra maheśvara pramātri*, and *Śiva pramātri*. This process is completely automatic, nothing is to be done. In all of the earlier processes, the fifteen fold process, the thirteen fold process, and even in the eleven fold process, *māyā* to a greater or lesser extent is present. In the nine fold process *māyā* has completely disappeared. This and the following processes have only to be done once. They are completely automatic. They are done only to strengthen your awareness. You want your awareness to be absolutely strengthened when you reach the state of Śiva.

After completing this nine fold process you must begin *saptatattvātmaviddhiḥ*, the seven fold process. This includes three *pramātrins*, three *pramātri śaktis*, and the object. The object in this process is *mantra pramātri* (*śuddhavidyā*) and the observer is *mantreśvara*. You will automatically travel from the *mantreśvara* state to *mantra maheśvara* and then to Śiva *pramātri*.

Next, you must take up *pañcatattvātmavidhiḥ*, the five fold process. Here there are two *pramātrins*, two *pramātri śaktis*, and the object. The object here is *mantreśvara* (*īśvara*) and the perceiver is *mantra maheśvara pramātri*. Here, you travel automatically from *mantra maheśvara pramātri* to Śiva *pramātri*.

The final process which you must undergo is *tritattvātmavidhiḥ*, the three fold process. The object in this process is *mantra maheśvara pramātri* (*sadāśiva*). Here the perceiver and the energy of perception is only one and that is Śiva. This is the last process because here there is only one

objective being and one subjective being. Śadāśiva is the
object and the perceiver is Śiva. "śiva sākṣāt na bhidyate".
"Upon realizing Śiva, no other process remains." There is no
one fold process. When you perceive the state of sadāśiva as
the object you are in the state of Śiva. No more rising can take
place. There is nowhere to rise to. You automaticaily become
that One Universal seated in that state of Śiva as observed and
as observer. Here, you rise from Śiva to Śiva, from transcendental being to transcendental being. This state is completely
full. Here, thisness is found in Śiva and Śiva is found in thisness. It is said

> abhedebhedanam bhedite ca
> antarānusaṁdhānena abhedanam /

> See duality in uniṫy and unity in duality

This is the actual state of Śaivism wherein you realize that
the point from which you have to start is the ending point, that
the existence of Śiva is the same at the starting point and at the
ending point. There is really no where to go and nothing to be
done. It is for the obtaining of this reality of Universal
Oneness that we are taught pañcadaśavidhih, the fifteen fold
process in the Mālinī Vijaya Tantra.

Chapter Ten

The Five Great Acts of Lord Śiva
Pañcakrityavidhiḥ

The five great acts of Lord Śiva are *sṛṣṭi*, the creative act, *sthiti*, the protective act, *samhāra*, the destructive act, *tirodhāna*, the act of enfolding or concealing His nature, *anugraha*, the act of unfolding or revealing His nature. Each of these acts are also accomplished by the individual soul. In the case of the individual, however, they are not called 'acts' they are called 'actions' because this kind of act is dependent to the will of God not to the will of the individual being. The individual being does not act according to his own will, he can not. He is dependent to the will of God, Lord Śiva. It is only God that is completely independent. There is a difference, therefore, between 'action' and 'act'. 'Action' is attributed to the individual soul and 'act' is attributed to Lord Śiva.

If you believe that because the individual soul does not perform 'acts' but only 'actions' and that he has no freedom and, therefore, he can not be held responsible for his actions you are wrong. The limited individual is responsible for his actions. He does have ego and feels that he is acting himself. When he feels that he is acting himself then he is responsible for his actions. If he were to feel that Lord Śiva is really the actor and that it is Lord Śiva that is acting, not himself, only then is he not responsible for his actions. But then, of course, he could do no wrong.

In the Kingdom of Spirituality Lord Śiva creates Masters and disciples through His fifth act, the act of grace (anugraha). This grace is nine fold and therefore He creates Masters and disciples in nine different ways.

The first and highest level of grace is called tīvratīvra śaktipāta. Tīvratīvra śaktipāta means 'Super Supreme Grace'. When Lord Śiva bestows on anyone super supreme grace then that person becomes perfectly self recognized. He knows his real nature completely and in perfection. At the same time, however, this kind of intense grace can not be resisted by his body and he throws away his body and is dead. This person becomes a Master, however, he accomplishes the act of his mastery secretly in the deserved hearts of disciples. He is not visible in this world. Only those that are deserving experience his subtle existence.

The second intensity of grace is called tīvramadhya-śaktipāta. This is 'Supreme Medium Grace'. The effect of this grace of Lord Śiva is that the recipient becomes completely and perfectly illumined, but he does not leave his body. He is said to be a prātibha guru, that is, a Master who is made not by another Master through that Master's initiation but by his self, by his own grace. He experiences spontaneous enlightenment. These particular Masters live in this world with their physical bodies for the upliftment of mankind.

The third intensity of grace is called tīvramandaśaktipāta which means 'Inferior Supreme Grace.' In him who has received this grace the desire appears for going to the feet of a spiritual Master. And the Master that he finds has received the second intensity of grace, tīvramadhyaśaktipāta. This Master is perfect. He is all knowing. There is no difference between this Master and Śiva. This Master does not initiate him, rather, he simply touches him with his divine hand, or gazes upon him, or embraces him, and at that very moment this disciple who is a recipient of medium supreme grace perfectly transcends individuality and enters into that supreme transcendental state without the need of practicing *japa* (recitation) or *dhyāna* (contemplation), etc. Although he still experiences pleasure and pain in his physical body it does not effect him as his being has become supreme.

That Master who has received this particular intensity of grace which is known as *Rudra śakti-samāveśaḥ* is called *Rudra śakti-samāviṣṭaḥ* because he has completely entered into the trance of *Rudra śakti*, the energy of Śiva. He exhibits five signs which can be observed by others. The first sign is his intense love for Lord Śiva. The second sign is that whenever he recites any mantra the *devatā* (deity) of that mantra appears to him at once without his having to wait. This is called *mantrasiddhiḥ*. The third sign which can be observed is that he has control over the five elements. The fourth sign is that whatever work he begins he completes that work without defect. And the fifth sign is that either he is a master of all the scriptures or he becomes a great poet.

Lord Śiva, through these three supreme intensities of grace, creates Masters in the kingdom of spirituality. With less intensities of grace Lord Śiva creates worthy disciples.

The fourth intensity of grace is called *madhyatīvara śaktipāta*. This is 'Medium Supreme Grace'. Through the effect of this intensity of grace the disciple reaches the feet of that Master who is absolutely perfect. But because the foundation established in the mind of this disciple is not quite completely perfect, the mere touch or glance of this perfect Master will not bring this disciple to enlightenment. He, therefore, initiates this disciple in the proper fashion by giving him a *mantra* and teaching him the proper way of treading. Through this initiation this disciple becomes enlightened, however, he is not completely satisfied with this enlightenment during the period of the existence of his physical body. At the time of his death though, when he leaves his physical body, he obtains completely satisfactory results from the earlier initiation he had received and becomes one with Śiva.

The fifth intensity of grace is called *madhyamadhya śaktipāta* which means 'Medium Middle Grace'. When Lord Śiva bestows this particular intensity of grace upon someone the intense desire for achieving the existence of Lord Śiva arises in this person's mind. At the same time, however, he does not want to ignore the enjoyments and pleasures of the world. He wants to enjoy worldly pleasure along with wanting to realize the existence of Lord Śiva. Yet the intensity of his desire is only for achieving Lord Śiva's state. So, although he is initiated by a Master and realizes his Real nature as Lord Śiva, his Real Self, and enjoys the bliss of that state while remaining in his physical body, simultaneously he also enjoys the pleasures of the world. But as these worldly pleasures, which take place in this mortal field of the universe, are not real pleasures, therefore, at the time of his leaving his physical body he enters into the Kingdom of Paradise *(svargaloka)* and enjoys all the worldly pleasures to his entire satisfaction. After he has satisfied his desire for worldly pleasures he does not come down again into this world but is again initiated by his Master, who is all pervading, while he remains in heaven. Through this initiation he becomes complete and realizes the reality of his Supreme Nature and from heaven itself he enters into the Kingdom of Lord Śiva and merges in Him completely.

The sixth intensity of grace is called *madhyamanda śaktipāta* which means 'Medium Inferior Grace'. The effect of this grace is very much like the effect of Medium Middle Grace, however, the difference lies in predominance. The effect of Medium Middle Grace is that in the mind of the disciple arises both the desire for attaining the State of Lord Śiva and the desire for experiencing worldly pleasures, however, the predominant desire is for attaining the State of Lord Śiva. The effect of Medium Inferior Grace is also that in the mind of this disciple arises both the desire for attaining the State of Lord Śiva and the desire for experiencing worldly pleasures, however, the predominant desire here is for experiencing worldly pleasures. Though he achieves Self Realization it is not complete because of the agitation he experiences for seeking worldly pleasures. So at the time of his leaving his physical body this intensity of grace carries him from this mortal world first to paradise where he enjoys the pleasures of the world. While in paradise, however, he does not gain the fitness to begin practicing for attaining the realization of his Self. He must, therefore, be again reborn and come down into this mortal field. And from that very birth he sentences his mind toward the fulfillment of his Self realization. Although his life in this mortal realm is very short as Lord Śiva wants to carry him quickly to His own State, yet he becomes absolutely complete in that short span of time and enters, in the end, into the Transcendental state of Śiva.

The above three medium intensities of grace take place in the field of aspirants living in the kingdom of *Śivadharma*. Those aspirants living in this field of *Śivadharma* have the tendency for achieving the state of Self Realization at least half hourly during the day and at least twice during the night. The remaining period they keep aside for worldly pleasures.

The following three inferior intensities of grace, *manda tīvra* (Inferior Supreme), *manda madhya* (Inferior Medium), and *manda manda* (Inferior Inferior), take place in the field of aspirants living in the kingdom of *lokadharmah*, the kingdom of worldly life. These aspirants have the desire for achieving the state of Lord Śiva, Self Realization, only when the pains and pressures of this world become too much to bear. At that moment they want to abandon everything and achieve Self

Realization, however, they are not able to and though they want to leave this worldly life they can not leave. These aspirants have more tendency for worldly pleasure and less tendency for realizing their Self. But, as the grace of Lord Śiva shines in them, in the end, which may take many lifetimes, they become one with the Supreme Being. This is the greatness of Lord Śiva's grace that in no matter what intensity His grace is with you it will carry you in the end to His Nature.

Chapter Eleven

The Five States of the Individual
Subjective Body

On the path of the thirty six elements only one universal subjective body is traveling in each element. There are not unlimited subjects traveling in these elements. All subjects *(jīvas)* are actually only the one subjective body of God. When He travels in the element of earth He becomes earth and loses His subjectivity of self. When He travels in the element of air He becomes air and loses His subjectivity of self. And this is the case with all of the thirty six elements. They are actually only one universal subjective body. This one subjective body travels, therefore, from earth to Śiva and when that subjective body reaches the state of Śiva that subjective body becomes Śiva.

As one universal subjective body travels in the thirty six elements the individual subjective body travels in five states. When this individual subjective body travels in objectivity and it becomes the object and ignores its subjective consciousness, this is one state. When it travels in the cognitive world and becomes one with that and loses consciousness of its subjectivity, this is the second state. When it travels in the subjective world without being conscious of that and becomes one with that unconscious subjectivity, this is the third state. When it travels in absolute subjective consciousness and it becomes that subjective consciousness this is the fourth state. And when it becomes fully established in that subjective consciousness, that is the fifth state. These five states, which comprise the individual subjective body, are called *jāgrat*, wakefulness, *svapna*, dreaming, *suṣupti*, deep sleep, *turya*, the fourth state, and *turyātītā*, beyond the fourth.

In *jāgrat*, wakefulness, the individual subjective body is traveling in the world of objectivity *(prameya)*, which comprises the world of elements, names, forms, words, and sounds. Here it loses consciousness of its subjectivity and becomes one with the objective world. In *svapna*, the dreaming state, the individual subjective body travels in the impressions *(saṁskāras)* of the objective world. Here it also loses the awareness of its subjective consciousness. It takes hold of these impressions and becomes one with the world of impressions. In *suṣupti*, deep dreamless sleep, it has entered a state of entire voidness *(śūnya)*. If it was previously traveling in the world of objectivity in the waking state, then upon entering deep sleep it loses consciousness of this objectivity and also of its subjectivity. If it was previously traveling in the world of impressions in the dreaming state then upon entering deep sleep it loses consciousness of these impressions. In deep sleep it is no longer aware of anything. The impressions of the objective world remain but these are as if dead. When it again returns from the state of deep sleep these impressions, which were seemingly dead, again come to life. And when, by the grace of a Master, this subjective body enters into subjective consciousness with full awareness, which subjective awareness is breakless awareness, and becomes fully illumined in its own Self, this state is called the fourth state, *turya*. And when this individual subjective body takes a firm hold of *turya* and does not for a moment lose consciousness of this state it is established in that state called *turyātītā*, above the fourth. It is completely established in its Self. Its awareness of Self is maintained constantly in wakefulness, dreaming, and deep sleep. It never loses its consciousness. Even at the time of death, because it lives in the body of consciousness, it remains completely Self aware.

Now I will explain to you how the four states of the individual, *jāgrat, svapna, suṣupti*, and *turya*, are found in each of these four states[1]. First let us take the state of *jāgrat*, wakefulness, and see how these four states exist in the waking state. The first state is *jāgrat jāgrat*, wakefulness in the world of wakefulness. Actually this objective wakefulness is the absence of wakefulness in the real sense because in this state you are given fully to the world of objectivity and you completely lose consciousness of your subjectivity. This is the state of complete objectivity. People who exist in this state are totally given to the objective world. They are never conscious of their self. They are absolutely unaware. They never ask the question, "Who am I?" When they observe any object such as a pot they become completely one with that object and lose consciousness that they are the observers. In Śaivism we call this state *abuddhaḥ*, the state of absolute unawareness.

The next state is called *jāgrat svapna*, dreaming in the state of wakefulness. When subjective consciousness enters into objective consciousness and then loses consciousness of that objectivity and lives, while in wakefulness, only in the impressions of objectivity, this is dreaming in the state of wakefulness. For instance, when, in the objective world, you look at a

---

1 *Turyātita*, beyond the fourth, is not found as mixed with any other state. *Turyātītā* is absolute. In *turyātītā* there is no contact of either objectivity or subjectivity. It is for this reason that only four different states are to be found in each of the four states of the individual subjective body. *Turyātītā* is not explained nor is it recognized in this context.

particular person and you are not aware of looking at at that person, then you are traveling in your own impressions, this is *jāgrat svapna*. In ordinary worldly life when a person is in the state of *jāgrat svapna* we say that he is 'daydreaming' or that he is 'lost in thought.' In our philosophy we call this state *budhāvasthā*, that state which has some awareness, some consciousness.

The next state in *jāgrat* is called *jāgrat suṣupti*, deep sleep in the state of wakefulness. When in the state of wakefulness that individual subjective body, both externally and internally, loses consciousness of the objective world and also loses consciousness of the world of impressions he is in the state of *jāgrat suṣupti*. Externally he is not experiencing the objective world and internally he is not experiencing the world of impressions. In our Śaivism this state is called *prabuddhaḥ*, "with consciousness," because he has reached very near to the Supreme Consciousness of Being.

The highest and most refined state in *jāgrat* is called *jāgrat turya*, the fourth state in the state of wakefulness. In this state, the individual subjective body, after losing consciousness of both external and internal objectivity, enters into some consciousness of Self, of Being. He is partly illuminated by that awareness of Self and he becomes quite aware internally of the consciousness of Self. He moves and travels in the objective world, and at the same time he resides in Self Consciousness. He does not lose hold of his internal subjective consciousness. In Śaivism *jāgrat turya* is called *suprabuddhaḥ*, absolutely full of awareness.

Also in the *svapna*, the state of dreaming, where you travel only in impressions, the four states of *jāgrat*, *svapna*, *suṣupti*, and *turya*, are to be found. *Svapna* is the state found in dreaming, in impressions, in memory, in madness, and in intoxication. The first state in *svapna* is known as *svapna jāgrat*, wakefulness in the state of dreaming. When the subjective body travels in impressions and is given to those impressions in the field of objectivity and at the same time loses consciousness of those impressions, this is the state of individuality called *svapna jāgrat*. Here, this individual sometimes travels in the waves of impressions and sometimes travels in the waves of objectivity. For example, if in a dream you see a pencil and then, when you look again, you see a knife in place of the pencil you are not conscious of this change. You do not ask the question, "Why is there now a knife where there once was a pencil?" Everything in this state, whether normal or abnormal, seems normal and ordinary to you. It is objective because you are given to objectivity and are lost in the object, which in this example is the pencil. The question, "How is this so" does not arise in your mind. This state in Śaivism is called *gatāgatam*, which means 'you come and you go', — sometimes it is a pencil and sometimes it is not a pencil.

The next state found in *svapna*, the dreaming state, is called *svapna svapna*, dreaming in the state of dreaming. In this state the individual subjective body travels only in the world of impressions without the least awareness of their connection of one to the other. You see a pencil, then you see a book, then you fly in the air, then you are driving a motor car and yet you are not aware of any of this. You feel that everything is perfectly alright. In our Śaivism this state is called *suvikṣiptam*, 'absolutely dispersed consciousness.' You travel here and there, you do this and see that, and yet you do not know anything.

The third state found in *svapna* is called *svapna suṣupti*, deep sleep in the state of dreaming. Sometimes in the dreaming state this subjective body, while traveling in the world of impressions and thoughts, also develops some awareness of subjectivity. If, for example, you were to see a pencil in a dream and then in the next moment you were to see a knife in place of the pencil, you would think and wonder why the pen-

cil has become a knife. You realize that you are not awake,
that you must be dreaming. You are traveling in subjectivity,
however, that subjectivity does not remain. Because this state
is *suṣupti* in the state of dreaming your subjective consciousness comes and goes. You question and argue and then you
forget, you lose this consciousness and are again traveling in
impressions. This state of individuality is called *saṁgatam*,
which means 'touched.' Here you experience the occasional
touch of consciousness.

The next and highest state in *svapna* is called *svapna
turya*, the fourth state in the state of dreaming. When you are in the
dreaming state and observe some particular object you perceive this particular object in the world of impressions. And
when at that very moment, while in the dreaming state, you
become aware, you become conscious that you are not awake,
that you are in the dreaming state and, by the grace of your
Master, you caste away the objective world of impressions and
enter into *samādhi*, this is the state of *svapna turya*. This state,
however, is not permanent. Again you fall into the dreaming
state full of impressions and begin to dream. Realizing that
you are again dreaming you enter again into *samādhi* and then
again another dream comes and takes you away. You move
from the dreaming state to *samādhi* and then back to the
dreaming state and again to *samādhi* and so forth. You are
incapable of maintaining that state of *samādhi*. This state is
known in Śaivism as *susamāhitam,* which means 'absolutely
aware, full of awareness.'

In *suṣupti*, deep sleep, the first state of these four states is
suṣupti jāgrat, wakefulness in the state of deep sleep. In this
state of deep sleep you lose all impressions and thoughts and
remain in absolute void *(śūnya)*. While remaining in this state
you are not aware and you do not taste its joy. For example, if
you have fallen into this state of dreamless sound sleep, where
you neither travel in objectivity nor in impressions, and when

you come out from that dreamless state someone were to ask you, "Where were you?" You would reply, *(nakiñcidjño'smi)* "I do not know anything." Sometimes upon coming out from deep sleep you realize that while you were asleep you did not know anything, however, you do know that you were peacefully happily sleeping, that it was absolutely peaceful. This experience "I was peacefully sleeping," does not occur in *suṣupti jāgrat* In *suṣupti jāgrat* you remember afterwards that you were experiencing nothing.

na kiñcidahamavediṣam
gāḍha mūḍho'hamasvāpsam

"I was asleep and I observed nothing."

In our Śaivism this state is called *uditaṁ,* full of rising. It is said to be full of rising because you have thrown away the world of impressions and entered into the negation of impressions. You are rising out of the world of impressions towards Śiva.

The next state in deep sleep is called *suṣupti svapna,* dreaming in the state of deep sleep. While in deep sleep you are traveling in the world of unconscious subjectivity. It is the world of subjectivity where subjectivity is absent from consciousness. In deep sleep there is no consciousness, no awareness of that subjectivity. You remain in that subjectivity but you do not know that you are in subjectivity. In the state of *suṣupti svapna,* however, you have some impression of being in subjectivity, there is some cognition of remaining in that subjectivity. In this state you are somewhat conscious that you are traveling in subjectivity. In Śaivism we call this state *vipulam,* which means 'gets nourished.' This means that the impression and awareness that you are traveling in the world of subjective consciousness gradually becomes stronger and stronger, it slowly increases.

The third state of deep sleep is called *suṣupti suṣupti*, deep sleep in the state of deep sleep. In this state, while you are traveling in the world of subjective consciousness, the impression, the faint idea that this is the world of subjective consciousness remains in the background throughout, without interruption. In the state of *suṣupti svapna* you also have some impression of remaining in subjectivity, however, it is an interrupted perception. Yet in both cases, in *suṣupti svapna* and in *suṣupti suṣupti*, where the impression, the faint idea that this is the world of subjective consciousness remains in the background, *suṣupti* is in predominance. This state, in which the subtle awareness that this is the world of subjective consciousness remains in uninterrupted continuity, is called in our Śaivism *śāntām*. *Śāntām* means "peaceful." This state is called *śāntām* because your awareness remains in the background in an absolutely peaceful state. There is no agitation in this state.

The fourth state of deep sleep is *suṣupti turya*, the fourth state in the state of deep sleep. In this state you travel in the world of subjective consciousness. You are aware of that subjective consciousness in continuation in the background and at the same time you experience the bliss of this state. In the state *suṣupti suṣupti* you do not experience the real bliss of this subjective state, you only experience its peace. Here, in *suṣupti turya*, you experience the positive bliss of this state. In this state you are entering into *samādhi* and yet consciousness still remains in the background. In our Śaivism we call this state *suprasannām* because this is that state in which you are absolutely full of bliss even though you are not fully aware of that bliss.[2]

---

2. uditaṁ vipulaṁ śāntaṁ suprasannamathāparam

Mālinī Vijaya Tantra: II;45

Let's turn now and look again at the three states of the individual subjective body. The word *jāgrat* refers to that state wherein one is full of awareness from his own point of view, from the point of view of individual consciousness, not from the point of view of subjective consciousness. It is worldly people that call this state *jāgrat* (waking). Yogins, on the other hand, have a different name for this state. Yogins feel that when you come in the state of objective consciousness you become one with objectivity. This state, therefore, is not actually the state of waking. It cannot be *jāgrat*. It is really the state of becoming one with objectivity. For this reason they have named this state as *piṇḍasthaḥ* where you become one with whatever you perceive. Enlightened souls *(jñānīs)* have another name for this state as they experience that in this state the Being of Śiva has expanded His Body of Consciousness in names, forms, space, and time. These *jñānīs* feel the consciousness of Śiva everywhere. It is for this reason that they call this state *sarvatobhadra*[3] which means 'everywhere divine.' For these enlightened souls wherever they go they feel the divinity of God Consciousness. Whenever they travel in the objective world, whether in name, form, space, time, whether walking or talking, whatever they may be doing, they are traveling in Absolute Consciousness.

The dreaming state is called *svapna*, (the absence of worldly activity) by worldly people because the outer objective world is absent in this state. Yogins, on the other hand, call this state *padastham* which means, 'being established where you are', because here you get established in your own point. Yogins find that *svapna* is a nearer way when entering into

---

3. sarvatobhadramāsīnaṁ
   sarvato vedyasattayā ॥

samādhi, when entering into the absolute. When you are in the
state of *jāgrat* you have to struggle to enter into the state of
samādhi. When you are in the state of *svapna* you only have to
struggle half as much. It is much easier to concentrate your
awareness in *svapna* than it is in *jāgrat*. Children exist primarily in *svapna*. If illuminating power is put in them by some
Master or greater soul they will enter into *samādhi* in an
instant. They have no external thoughts, they have only internal thoughts. They are very near to their own Self. *Jñānīs* call
the state of *svapna*, *vyāpti*, which means 'pervasion', because
in the dreaming state they pervade everything and they know
that they are pervading. They pervade their own body, the
motor car that they are dreaming they are driving, the road that
they are dreaming they are driving on, and the place that they
are dreaming they are going to. The reality is that none of
these objects are produced by any outside agency. They are all
existing in their own self.[4]

Worldly people call the state of deep sleep *suṣupti* (asleep)
because they have no knowledge of objectivity in this state. In
this state there is no objectivity and there are no impressions.
This state is *tūṣṇīmbhāva* which means 'absolute silence.' For
them it is an appeased state. They feel that after leaving this
state they are more peaceful. They find this state to be nourish-
ing. Yogins, on the other hand, feel that in this state of sound
sleep they become attached to their own nature. This state for
Yogins is full of consciousness while this state for worldly
people is full of unconsciousness. Yogins, therefore, call this
state *rūpastha*, which means 'established in one's own Self',
because here they are established in their own Consciousness.

---

4. The *Jñānī* does not desire to direct his actions in a dream. A *Jñānī* is
   desireless. A *Jñānī* does not desire he just moves. It is Universal Will that
   acts. The *Jñānī* is touched with Universal Will.

Jñānīs call this state *mahāvyāpti* (the great pervasion) because here they find that there is absolutely no limitation of objectivity or impressions.

From the Trika Śaivaite point of view predominance is given to the three energies of Śiva, *parā śakti*, the supreme energy, *parāparā śakti*, medium energy, and *aparā śakti*, inferior energy. The kingdom of *aparā śakti*, the lowest energy, is found in wakefulness and dreaming. The kingdom of *parāparā śakti*, the medium energy, is established in the state of sound sleep. And lastly the kingdom of *parāśakti*, the supreme energy, is found in the state of *turya*.

The state of *turya* is above the state of *pramātri*. It is called the state of *pramiti*. *Pramiti* is that state where subjective consciousness prevails without the agitation of objectivity. Where the agitation of objectivity is also found in subjective consciousness then that is the state of *pramātri*. For example, when a person is lecturing on some points and he is full of those objects that he is explaining, this is the state of *pramātri*. And when that same experiencer is without the agitation of lectures and there is no objective world before him, this is the state of *pramiti*. The state of *pramiti* is without any object at all. In other words, when he is residing in his own Nature, that subjective consciousness is called the state of *pramiti*.

The state of *turya* is said to be the penetration of all energies simultaneously, not in succession. All of the energies are residing there but not in manifestation. They are all together without distinction. *turya* is called *savyāpārā* because all of the energies get their power to function in that state. At the same time this state is known as *anāmayā* because it remains unagitated by all of these energies.

There are three names attributed to this state by worldly people, by yogins, and by illuminated humans (*jñānīs*). Worldly people call it *turya*, which means 'the fourth.' They use this name because they have no descriptive name for this state. They are unaware of this state, have not experienced it and, therefore, simply say that it is the fourth state. Yogins have attributed the name *rūpātītā* to this state because this state has crossed 'the touch of one's self' and is 'the establishment of one's self.' The touch of one's self was found in sound sleep, however, the establishment of this takes place in *turya*. For illuminated humans, *jñānīs*, the entire universal existence is found in this state of *turya*, collectively, as undifferentiated, in the state of totality. There is no succession here. *Jñānīs*, therefore, call this state *pracyaya*.[5]

Now I'll explain the names given to the states of *turya jāgrat*, *turya svapna*, and *turya suṣupti*. Only these three states are possible in *turya*. As *turya* cannot be divided *turya turya* is not possible. The preceding states of individual subjective consciousness, *jāgrat*, *svapna*, and *suṣupti*, each have four aspects, the state of *turya* has only three.

The state of *turya jāgrat* exists when the consciousness of *turya* is not vividly manifested. Here the consciousness of *turya* is in a subconscious state, it is unmanifestly found in the background. In this state, though strong consciousness exists, it is not manifested totally, it is yet to be manifested. In the state of *turya svapna* the consciousness of *turya* is more vividly manifested. Consciousness is stronger here. And in the state of *turya suṣupti* the consciousness of *turya* is most vivid. Here consciousness is the strongest. The state of *turya jāgrat* is called *manonmanam* 'beyond the span of the mind', because it is that state where the mind has taken rise in mindlessness, complete thoughtlessness. The state of *turya svapna* is named *anantam* which means 'unlimited' because here is found the unlimitedness of the Self. There is no limitation of Being here.

---

5. *Pracyaya* means literally "multitude" and refers to the undifferentiated totality of universal existence.

This is the state of unlimited Being. *turya suṣupti* is called *sarvārtham*. *Sarvārtham* means that in this state, although you are unlimited, yet you find existing here all of the limitations of the universe.[6]

Turyātīta is that state which is the absolute fullness of Self. It is filled with all consciousness and bliss. It is really the last and the supreme state of the Self. You not only find this state in *samādhi*, you also find this state in each and every activity of the world. There is no possibility in this state for the practice of yoga. If you can practice yoga then you are not in *turyātīta*. In yoga there is the intention of going somewhere. Here, there is no where to go, nothing to achieve. As concentration does not exist here the existence of the hand of yoga is not possible.

There are only two names actually attributed to this state of *turyātīta*, one given by worldly people and one by *Jñānīs*. Worldly people, because they know nothing about this state, call it *turyātīta*, which means 'that state which is beyond the fourth.' *Jñānīs*, on the other hand, have also named this state. They call it *mahāpracaya*[7] which means 'the unlimited and unexplainable supreme totality.' Yogins do not actually attribute any name to this state because they have no knowledge of this state. It is completely outside of their experience. Yogins have though, through the use of their imagination and through guesswork, imagined one name which might be

---

6. manonmanamanantaṁ ca
   sarvārthamiti bhedataḥ

   Mālinī Vijaya Tantra: II;46

7. mahāpracayamicchanti
   turyātītaṁ vicakṣaṇāḥ ||

   Mālinī Vijaya Tantra: II;38

appropriate for this state. They say that it is *satatoditam*[8] which means 'that state which has no pause, no break.' It is a breakless and unitary state. In *samādhi* it is there. When *samādhi* is absent it is there. In the worldly state it is there. In the dreaming state it is there. And in the state of deep sleep it is there. In each and every state of the individual subjective body it is there.

I have explained the nature of these five states of individual subjectivity from the Trika point of view. In the Pratyabhijñā Philosophy the Masters of the Pratyabhijñā School have also explained and defined these five states. Their definitions of *jāgrat*, *svapna*, and *susupti* seem to differ somewhat from that given by the Trika Śaivaites. Their explanations of *turya* and *turyātīta*, however, are the same.

The masters of the Pratyabhijñā School say that when you remain in that state where your consciousness is directed towards objectivity *(bahirvritti)* and you are no longer in your own subjective consciousness, that state is to be known as *jāgrat*. When you remain only in the sphere of impressions and thoughts *(samkalpa nirmāna)*, that state is to be known as *svapna*. And when there is the absolute destruction of all impressions, thoughts, and consciousness *(pralayopamam)*, when you are absolutely dead in your own self, that state is to be known as *susupti*.

Abhinavagupta the greatest Master of Śaivism and the greatest philosopher the world has ever known gives the general definition of these states so that the student will know that there is really no difference at all between the Trika Śaivaite and the Pratyabhijñā points of view. He explains that when

---

8. turyātīte bheda ekah
   satatodita ityayam ||

Tantrāloka: X;283

there is vividness of objectivity that is the state of *jāgrat*.
When the vividness of objectivity is shaky and unstable, that is
svapna. When the vividness of objectivity is gone completely
that is *suṣupti*. When super observation is found by some
observing agency that is *turya*. And when that objectivity is
individually dead and found full of life in totality that is
turyātīta.

Chapter Twelve

The Five Fold Contacts
of Masters and Disciples

In this universe from times immemorial the initiation of Masters has taken place from the state of Lord Śiva up to the state of mortal beings. This contact of the Master with the disciple takes place in five different ways. The highest contact of the Master with the disciple is called *mahān sambandhaḥ* (the great contact). This highest contact took place in the very beginning of the manifestation of the universe. In this case Lord Śiva became the Master and Sadāśiva was the disciple. Next, after this highest contact, a lower contact took place which is called *antarāla sambandhaḥ*. This is the contact of the Master who is residing in the state of *Sadāśiva* with that disciple who is residing in the state of Anantabhaṭṭāraka. Then the third contact between Master and disciple took place. This third contact is called *divyasambandhaḥ* which means 'divine contact'. It took place when the Master was at the state of Anantabhaṭṭāraka with that disciple who was in the state of Śrīkaṇṭhanātha. The fourth contact is called *divyādivya-sambandha*, which means 'that contact which is partly divine and partly not divine'. In this fourth contact Śrīkaṇṭhaḥ took the place of divinity as the Master and Sanatkumāra Ṛiṣi took the place of being the disciple. And lastly, the fifth contact of Masters and disciples took place with the Masters residing in the place of Sanatkumāra Ṛiṣi and the disciples as mortal beings *(manuṣya)*. This fifth contact is called *adivya sambandha* which means, 'that contact which is not divine.'

This fifth contact of Masters and disciples has occurred many times in this universe. In the latest movement of this contact the Master was Durvāsā Ṛiṣi, as he was from the school of thought of Sanatkumāra Ṛiṣi, and the disciple was Tryambakanātha.

Although our Kashmir Śaivism recognizes these five fold contacts of Masters and disciples, yet it explains that only that initiation is a real initiation where the contact of the Master and the disciple takes place in such a way that at the time of initiation the Master is united with the disciple and the disciple is united with the Master. In this real initiation the Master becomes one with the disciple and the disciple becomes one with the Master. You should understand, however, that for this supreme contact to take place the disciple should never find any fault in his Master or his Master's activity. If he does, then he is lost. This kind of initiation can take place in any state of these five contacts. It is the real supreme contact. It is even above *mahānsambandhaḥ* (the great contact) and is called *parasambandhaḥ* (the supreme contact). It is that contact by which all contacts become divine. The real theory of our Śaivism is that this contact, which is the supreme contact, must take place between each and every Master and each and every disciple. When this occurs then that initiation is a real initiation.

Chapter Thirteen

The Birth of the Tantras

In the beginning of *satyuga*[1] Lord Śiva appeared in the form of Svacchandanātha. As Svacchandanātha He appeared with five heads and eighteen arms. His five heads came into manifestation through his five great energies, *cit śakti*, all consciousness, *ānanda śakti*, all bliss, *icchā śakti*, all will, *jñāna śakti*, all knowledge, and *kriyā śakti*, all action. And these five energies, which appeared in His five mouths and which are known as *īśāna*, *Tatpuruṣa*, *Sadyojāta*, *Vāmadeva*, and *Aghora*, because of the grace *(anugrahaḥ)*[2] of Lord Śiva, experienced the sensation of illuminating the Universe.

---

1. *satyuga* is the first age of the four ages *satyuga, tretāyuga, dvāparayuga,* and *kālīyuga*. These comprise the four fold cyclical life of the universe.

2. The grace *(anugraha)* of Lord Śiva is manifested through His five acts, creation, protection, destruction, concealing, and revealing. In these five acts Lord Śiva creates the universe, protects it, destroys it, conceals it in His own Nature, and illuminates it. In fact Lord Śiva creates, protects, destroys, and conceals this universe only to illuminate it.

You see, Lord Śiva wanted to enlighten the universe by manifesting the existence of the *Tantras*. In order to accomplish this He manifested these *Tantras* through his five mouths. Initially each of these mouths, *īśāna*, *Tatpuruṣa*, *Sadyojāta*, *Vāmadeva*, and *Aghora*, created one *Tantra*. Then two mouths joined together and created one *Tantra* from each combination of two mouths. And then three mouths joined together created one *Tantra* from each combination of three mouths. And then four mouths joined together, and then five mouths, and these combinations of mouths produced all of the *Tantras* of our Śaivism.

These *Tantras* are manifested in three ways. Initially ten *Tantras* came into existence which were dualistic *(dvaita)* and are called *Śiva Tantras*. These *Tantras*, which are not connected with Kashmir Śaivism, are filled with dualism. Then eighteen *Tantras* came into existence which were filled with that thought which is monistic dualism *(bhedābheda)*. These *Tantras* are called *Rudra Tantras*. And finally these five mouths came into existence in such a way that each and every mouth was simultaneously filled with the other four mouths. Here four of the five energies were inserted into the fifth energy in such a way that it became full with all five energies. No one energy was in predominance, all were equal. And this happened to each and every energy. Simultaneously, from these mouths, came out *Bhairava Tantras* which are filled only with monistic thought *(abheda)*. These *Bhairava Tantras*, which are the *Tantras* connected with Kashmir Śaivism, are sixty four in number.

In *Bhairava Tantras* Lord Śiva is shown to be in predominance everywhere, in Śiva and in all of His energies He is there in Fullness. He is equally present in everything and everywhere. You cannot say that something is closer to Him and something else is farther away. In everything He is there fully and completely.

Initially this monistic *Tantra*, in the form of one Supreme Consciousness and Bliss, was not manifested in will, imagination, or words, rather it was felt and observed by Lord Śiva Himself at the start of the illuminating energy. At this point the manifestation of this *Tantra* resided in Lord Śiva's innermost speech *parāvāk* (supreme speech). In this supreme speech of Lord Śiva the creation of *vācya* and *vācaka*, master and disciple, was not yet felt as being differentiated. They resided in His own Being as undifferentiated. In the next movement of illuminating energy the manifestation of the *Tantras* were held in his second speech *paśyantī*. At this stage also, these *Tantras* were still undifferentiated and were one with His Supreme Will. In the next movement of illuminating energy these *Tantras* were held in His third speech *madhyamā vāk*. Here they became differentiated and were manifested internally only in thought but not in words. And in the final movement of illuminating energy these *Tantras* were held in His fourth speech *vaikharī vāk* where they came out through His five mouths in differentiation as words, sentences, and verses.

In the three *yugas* (ages), *satyuga*, *tretāyuga*, *dvāparayuga*, Masters and disciples were initiated verbally, not in writing, and not through the learning of words and sentences. The power of memory in them was so great that they remembered everything instantaneously. There was no need for them to write anything down or to refer to books and papers. The Masters and disciples were very great in these three *yugas*.

When *Kaliyuga* occurred these Masters and disciples were so disappointed that they hid themselves in unknown places in order to avoid the touch of the worldly people living at that time. Because of this, the theory of *Bhairava Tantras* and Kashmir Śaivism was lost. Lord Śiva, however, is always willful to illuminate the universe and so He reappeared in this world at Kailāśa mountain not in the form of Svacchandanātha with five mouths but in the form of Śrīkanṭhanātha. And in the form of Śrīkanṭhanātha He again taught the theory of *Bhairava Tantras* to the sage Durvāsā Ṛiṣi who was *ūrdhvaretah*, which means 'one who's power of sex is preserved', and who was, therefore, a *brahmacārī* (celibate). When Śrīkanṭhanātha initiated him at Kailāśa mountain Śrīkanṭhanātha told him that he was to expand the thought of *Bhairava Tantras* in all of the universe without restriction to caste, colour, or creed. After Śrīkanṭhanātha taught Durvāsā Ṛiṣi in this manner he disappeared into the ether.

Durvāsā Ṛiṣi, after meditating completely for acquiring a real and fit disciple for initiation, became disappointed. He could not find anyone in this world fit to be initiated. His initiation was a practical initiation because while initiating someone in the thought of *Bhairava Tantras* simultaneously he initiated him in the practical side of this thought. And this practical initiation manifested itself immediately without the disciples having to do any practice or yoga. This disciple would become instantaneously enlightened. As he could not find a disciple fit for initiation he created out of his mental power one mind born son. This mind born son was called Tryambakanātha. Durvāsā Ṛiṣi completely initiated Tryambakanātha in the way of *Bhairava Tantras*. Afterwards he created two more mind born sons Āmardakanātha and Śrīnātha. He initiated his son Āmardakanātha in the dualistic *Śiva Tantras* and he initiated his other son Śrīnātha in the monodualistic *Rudra Tantras*. All of this was done by Durvāsā Ṛiṣi for the upliftment of mankind.

For the upliftment of women Durvāsā Ṛiṣi created one mind born daughter and she was called Ardhatryambakā.[3] As Kashmir Śaivism does not recognize women to be in a state of

---

3. She was called Ardhatryambaka (one-half Tryambaka) because in India and Kashmir the daughter is considered to be only one-half the property of her father.

degradation Durvāsā Ṛiṣi initiated her completely in the monistic thought of *Bhairava Tantras*. As this view, that women are not in a state of degradation, is not held by the other two schools of Śaivism, the dualistic and monodualistic schools, Durvāsā Ṛiṣi created only one mind born daughter. His daughter Ardhatryambaka's teaching is known as the Ardhatryambaka school of *Bhairava Tantras*. But as the continuity of the Ardhatryambaka school manifested itself secretly in this *Kaliyuga* from one woman to another there is no history of this school.

Durvāsā Ṛiṣi's son Tryambakanātha, the founder of the monistic school of Śaivism, was also a celibate *(brahmacārī)*. According to the way of the sage Durvāsā Ṛiṣi he also created one mind born son and named him Tryambakāditya, which means 'the expansion of Tryambakanātha.' After initiating him completely in *Bhairava Tantras* Tryambakanātha entered a cave which is known as Tryambaka Guhā (cave) and disappeared. Tryambakanātha's son Tryambakāditya also created one mind born son and after initiating him, Tryambakāditya disappeared into the ether.[4]

In this manner fifteen *siddhas* were created by mind. When, however, the fifteenth *siddha* attempted to create a mind born son he was not successful. It is said that this fifteenth *siddha* was not fully introverted, that side by side he was also given to worldly pleasures. Because of this subtle impurity *(āṇava mala)* he was not successful in creating a mind born son. After sitting in long meditation he found in this world a girl with all good qualities and so he went to her father and made arrangements to marry this girl. After marriage they created one son

---

4. These sages were not born with sex they were 'mind born'. As they were *siddhas*, which are spiritual beings without any experience of physical limitations, they did not die, they simply disappeared.

who was called Saṁgamāditya and who, by his will, came to the valley of Kashmir and found Kailāsa mountain. S- aṁgamāditya, like his father, married and produced one son named Varṣāditya whom he initiated completely in the thought of the monistic *Bhairava Tantras*. Varṣāditya also married and produced one son named Aruṇāditya whom he initiated fully. Aruṇāditya married and created one son named Ānanda whom he initiated and who was also completely informed practically in Śaivism.

This sage Ānanda was the father of Somānandanātha, the originator of the Pratyabhijñā School of Śaivism and the author of the *"Śiva Dṛṣṭi"*. Up to the time of Somānandanātha the initiation into the monistic thought of *Bhairava Tantras* took place from father to son. From Somānandanātha onwards this initiation took place from Master to disciple. Somānandanātha was the Master of Utpaladeva. Utpaladeva was the Master of Lakṣmaṇagupta. And Lakṣmaṇagupta was a Master of our great Abhinavagupta who was in the line of Atrigupta.

Now I will explain to you how this Atrigupta, a great schol- ar of Kashmir Śaivism, came from India to live in the Kashmir Valley. After he moved to Kashmir there was no authority on Kashmir Śaivism left in India. From this time forward the teaching of the thought of *Bhairava Tantras* is called Kashmir Śaivism and this teaching has continued to remain centered only in the Kashmir Valley. Otherwise, these *Bhairava Tantras* are all pervading throughout the whole world, howev- er, they began in the Kashmir Valley, resided there, and are still alive there today.

During his reign, the king Lalitāditya traveled to India from Kashmir where in Antarvedi, a track of land in Madhya Pradesh which lies between the Yamuna and Ganges rivers, he discovered this great Śaiva teacher Atrigupta. Lalitāditya was deeply impressed by the scholarship and practical way of

Atrigupta and requested him to accompany him to the Kashmir Valley. Atrigupta agreed and upon reaching Kashmir was given the old palace of Pravarasena to live in as this palace was very near to the palace of the king Lalitāditya. After some centuries in the house of Atrigupta, Varāhagupta was born. He is the father of Narasimhagupta and Narasimhagupta is the father of our great Abhinavagupta. Although Abhinavagupta had many disciples, both men and women, his chief disciple was Kṣemarāja and the chief disciple of Kṣemarāja was Yogarāja. After many centuries in the Kashmir Valley Svāmī Ram came into this physical body. His chief disciple was Svāmī Mahatābakak and I am the disciple of Svāmī Mahatābakak.

Chapter Fourteen

Mokṣa in Kashmir Śaivism & Indian Philosophy

The view that ignorance is the cause of bondage and perfect knowledge is the cause of freedom *(mokṣa)* is commonly accepted by all Indian philosophers. Yet, in reality, these philosophers have not completely understood the reality of knowledge and ignorance.

The Vaiṣṇavites, for example, believe that liberation *(mokṣa)* from repeated births and deaths occurs when you are united with *parāprakṛti*.[1] And this union with *parāprakṛti*

---

1. *Prakṛti* is explained in the *śāstras* (scriptures) in two ways. *Aparā prakṛti,* which is said to be eight fold, is the combination of the five great elements along with mind, intellect, and ego.

> pañcemāni mahābāho
> kāraṇāni nibodha me I
> sāṁkhye kṛtānte proktāni
> siddhaye sarvakarmaṇām II
>
> *Bhagavadgītā XVIII:13*

Parāprakṛti is that energy of being which governs and holds all the activities and conceptions of this universe.

will take place only when you observe in your understanding that the differentiatedness of this universe is unreal. Then all attachments, pleasures, and pains will come to an end and you will be established in your own real nature. It is this establishment which, from their point of view, is called *moksa*.

The Advaita Vedāntins, on the other hand, have concluded that in the real sense *moksa* is only bliss *(ānanda)* and nothing else. They say that when you are residing in the field of ignorance *(samsāra)* you become the victim of the five fold veils, *avidyā* (ignorance), *asmitā* (ego), *rāga* (attachment), *dvesa* (hatred), and *abhinivesa* (attachment to your own conception). These coverings, which are the cause of your remaining in *samsāra*, should be removed by the practice of *tattvajñāna*. In this practice you must mentally negate all that is not your own real nature by thinking, *neti, neti,* 'I am not this, I am not this.' So here you practice thinking, "I am not the physical body, I am not the subtle body, I am not the mind, I am not the life essence *(prāna)*." You must negate all outside elements. And when you reside completely in your own nature, which is that which remains after you negate all outside elements, that knowledge, from their point of view, is called *moksa*.

The tradition of Buddhist philosophers, who are known as the *Vijñānavādins,* accept that you are liberated only when your mind is completely detached from all attachments to objectivity, pleasure, pain, and sorrow. They argue that the mind must remain only as mind, pure and perfect mind, because for them the mind is actually pure, filled with light, and detached from all worldly things. It is when the mind becomes attached to worldly things such as thoughts, pleasures, and pains, that you are carried to *samsāra*. And when these attachments are cancelled and the mind becomes pure then you are liberated.

The philosophers from the *Vaibhāsika* tradition hold that liberation is attained by deleting the chain of thoughts just like the flame of a lamp is extinguished. When a lamp is burning we experience the existence of the flame. When, however, the flame is extinguished it does not go anywhere, it does not go into the earth, or into the ether. When the flame is extinguished it simply disappears. And the extinguishing of the flame takes place when the oil of the lamp is exhausted. In the same way, when a yogī has crossed over all the pleasures and pains of the world those pleasures and pains do not go anywhere, they simply disappear. This yogī, who has extinguished the flame of the chain of thoughts by exhausting the wax of the five *kleśas*[2], enters in the supreme and perfect peace which is, from their point of view, liberation.

From the Śaivaite point of view these philosophical traditions remain either in *apavedyapralayākala* or in *savedyapralayākala*. They do not go beyond these states. *Apavedyapralayākala* is that state of *pralayākala* where there is no objectivity. *Savedyapralayākala* is that state of *pralayākala* where there is some impression of objectivity. As an example take the state of deep sleep. When you wake up from deep sleep and subsequently think, "I was sleeping and I didn't know anything," that is the state of *apavedyapralayākala*. And when you wake up from the state of deep sleep and subsequently think, "I was sleeping peacefully without dreaming," that is the state of *savedyapralayākala* because you experienced that it was a sweet sleep and so "sweetness" is the object for you in this state. Śaiva philosophy does not recognize the theories of these philosophies concerning *mokṣa* because in fact the yogins of these traditions do not move above the

---

2. *kleśas*, which means literally, "pains, misfortune," are afflictions which delude you and lead you astray. In Yoga philosophy these afflictions are five fold, *avidyā* (ignorance), *asmitā* (ego), *rāga* (attachment), *dveṣa* (hatred), and *abhiniveṣa* (attachment to your own conception).

pralayākala state and are not, therefore, situated in real *mokṣa*.
Our Śaivism explains that *jñāna* (knowledge) is knowing
one's own nature which is all Being *(sat)*, all consciousness
(cit), and all bliss *(ānanda)*. *Ajñāna* (ignorance) is ignoring
this nature and this is the cause of this *saṁsāra* which carries
one in the field of repeated births and deaths.

Kashmir Śaivism explains that ignorance *(ajñāna)* is of two
kinds, *pauruṣa ajñāna* and *bauddha ajñāna*. *Pauruṣa ajñāna*
is that kind of ignorance wherein one is unaware of realizing
their own nature in *samādhi*. This kind of ignorance is
removed by the grace of Masters and by meditating upon ones
own Self. And when this ignorance is removed you are situated in the real knowledge of Śaivism, which is all being, all
consciousness, all bliss. This kind of knowledge is called *pauruṣa jñāna*. When you possess *pauruṣa jñāna* you realize your
nature of Self perfectly.

Bauddha ajñāna (intellectual ignorance) occurs only when
you are completely ignorant of the philosophical truth of the
monistic thought of Śaivism. And *bauddha ajñāna* is removed
by studying those monistic Śaiva texts which explain the reality of the Self. In reality, therefore, these texts are the cause of
your being carried from *bauddha ajñāna* to *bauddha jñāna*.
Bauddha jñāna, therefore, is intellectual and is developed
through the intellect. *Pauruṣa jñāna*, on the other hand, is
practical and is developed through practice. *Pauruṣa jnana* is
predominant over *bauddha jñāna* because when you possess
only *pauruṣa jñāna* even then you are liberated in the real
sense and attain liberation. In this case, however, liberation is
attained only after leaving your body. When, however, at the
same time you also attach *bauddha jñāna* to *pauruṣa jñāna*,
which means that on the one hand you practice on your own
Being and on the other hand you go into the depth of the philosophical thought of the monistic Śaiva texts and elevate your
intellectual being, then you become a *jīvanmukta*, one who is

liberated while living. If, however, you possess only *bauddha jñāna* and not *pauruṣa jñāna* then you will not attain liberation either at the time of death or while living in the body. *Bauddha jñāna* without *pauruṣa jñāna* is useless and will not take you anywhere. The study of texts shines perfectly only when there is practical knowledge at the same time. Without practical knowledge philosophical study is useless. *Bauddha jñāna* will bear fruit only when *pauruṣa jñāna* is present and not otherwise.

If an aspirant is only attached to practical knowledge and not to theoretical knowledge, believing that the only real knowledge is practical knowledge which is the realizing of ones own nature, then he is incorrect from a Śaiva point of view. If only *pauruṣa jñāna* is cultivated and *bauddha jñāna* is totally ignored then there is every possibility that *pauruṣa jñāna* may decrease day by day, slowly fading away so that in the end it does not remain at all. It is the greatness of *bauddha jñāna* that with its power it firmly establishes *pauruṣa jñāna*. In this respect, therefore, *bauddha jñāna* is more predominant than *pauruṣa jñāna*.

In our Śaivism it is said that when you go in search of a Master so that you can be initiated you should first seek that Master who is full of both *bauddha jñāna* and *pauruṣa jñāna*. Finding him you should consider him as a real Master. If in this world such a complete Master is not to be found then you should seek that Master who is full only with *bauddha jñāna*. He is to be preferred over that Master who is filled only with *pauruṣa jñāna* because intellectually he will carry you by and by to the end point. That Master who only resides in *pauruṣa jñāna* would not ultimately be successful in carrying you to that which you seek.

Chapter Fifteen

Kashmir Śaivism & Advaita Vedānta

Although the main principle of both Kashmir Śaivism and Vedānta is monism *(advaita)*, pure monism, yet there are many important differences in their thinking. For example, Vedānta teaches that *karmayoga* means yoga in action. They believe that you must practice *nihṣkāma karmayoga* which means that you are to do all the actions of the world without asking for their reward. They say that by acting in this way you are carried towards the existence of the Real Being, the Real Nature of Self. From our Kashmir Śaiva point of view, however, *karmayoga* means something else. It does not mean doing all of the activities of the world. Yoga in action is pure yoga and nothing else. Pure yoga is onepointedness, and this onepointedness must be developed in three ways. You must develop onepointedness in the existence of your being. This is onepointedness in the state of *parā vāk* (supreme speech). You must also develop onepointedness in the state of *madhyamā vāk* (medium speech). And finally you must develop onepointedness in the state of *vaikharī vāk* (inferior speech), in the state of ordinary speech.

In Śaivism we begin with the central way, the way of *madhyamā vāk*. Kashmir Śaivism explains that yoga in action means that when you are seated in a bus, or when you are walking on the road, you must observe silence. Walk silently, sit in the bus silently. Do not talk to anybody. Continue your practice of contemplating Lord Śiva as you were instructed by your Master without talking to anybody. This is how you must begin. It is not possible at first to practice yoga while talking. In the beginning you have to start with silence.

This yoga in action is tremendously powerful. For example, if you were to continue your practice of contemplation for just fifteen minutes while walking the fruit will be the same as the fruit you would acquire if you were to continuously practice contemplation in your meditation room for two or even three years. This is because yoga in action makes your practice of contemplation more firm, more solid, more substantial. This is why Kashmir Śaivism puts stress on yoga in action, and not on that yoga which is inactive yoga.

In the practice of yoga in action in *madhyamā vāk* you begin with silence. And when you rise from *madhyamā* you will rise in the *parā* state of Śiva. This *parā* state will occur, however, only when you have completed your activity. For example, while practicing your contemplation you take a ten mile walk, five miles going and five miles coming, after which you return to your home where you sit in meditation. At this point you will enter automatically in the *parā* state of yoga in action and this will carry you rapidly to that state of Transcendental Being. You must enter into the *parā* state of yoga in action automatically. You cannot make it happen. If it does not happen then you will have to begin again practicing contemplation while in action. It is the strength of yoga in action that you enter into the *parā* state of yoga. If your contemplation while in action is spontaneous and breakless, then you will enter automatically into the *parā* state of yoga. If, on the other hand, your contemplation breaks at any time while practicing while in action then when you sit for meditation, contemplation on *para* will not take place and you will have to begin again. This is called *karmayoga*.

When you are established in the yoga of action in *parā vāk* then after some time you have to travel from *parā vāk* to *vaikharī vāk*. Practicing yoga in action in *vaikharī vāk* means that you are to remain established in your own Being while talking, while laughing, while doing all of the actions of the world. This kind of yoga in action in *vaikharī vāk* is not possible unless yoga in action in *madhyamā vāk* and yoga in action in *parā vāk* are complete. The sign of their being complete is that whenever you practice yoga in action in *madhyamā vāk* and afterwards you sit and practice you enter into *parā vāk*, you are inside, residing in your own Nature. Establishing yoga in action in *vaikharī vāk* is the completion of the course of yoga in action. Here you remain established in your own Being in all the activities of the world. It is said that Lord Krisna was perfectly established in yoga in action in *vaikharī*. He was very active, doing everything while remaining established in His own Nature.

The first difference, therefore, between Kashmir Śaivism and Vedānta is in their different understanding of *karmayoga*. This difference, as you have seen, is very great with the Vedāntins believing that *karmayoga* means doing all actions without asking for their reward and our Kashmir Śaivism teaching that yoga in action means doing all actions while maintaining a breakless contemplation of God.

Another of the differences to be found in the understanding of Kashmir Śaivism and Vedānta concerns the existence of individual being and Universal Being. The Vedāntins explain that individual being is manifested only when Universal Being is reflected in the mirror of the individual intellect. They say that Universal Being is reflected in the intellect *(buddhi)* and that reflection becomes the existence of the individual being *(jīva)*. Kashmir Śaivism, however, does not recognize this explanation, arguing that it is without any basis. As Universal Being is absolutely pure and perfect and individual being is filled with imperfections *(malas)* and covered by veils, it is not *buddhi* that will take the reflection of Universal Being rather it is Universal Being that will take the reflection of *buddhi*. It is the purer and more refined reality which will take the reflection of that which is less pure and refined and not the other way around. *Buddhi* cannot hold Universal Being. Kashmir Śaivism explains that when Śiva is reflected by His pure will in the mirror of his freedom *(svātantrya)* this is the existence of the universe and the existence of individual being.

Furthermore, in the theory of the Vedāntins it is not clearly explained how, if the world were not existing, *buddhi*, in which Lord Śiva is to be reflected, could exist at all? How could the intellect *(buddhi)* exist before the existence of the world? Therefore, individual being is the reflection of Lord Śiva in His *svātantrya śakti*. This is the existence of the universe.

The third area of difference in understanding between Kashmir Śaivism and Vedānta concerns the essence, the substance, the basis of this universe. Vedānta holds that this universe is untrue, unreal. It does not really exist. It is only the creation of illusion *(māyā)*. Concerning this point Kashmir Śaivism argues that if Lord Śiva is real then how could an unreal substance come out from something that is real. If Lord Śiva is real then His creation is also real. Why should it be said that Lord Śiva is real and His creation is an illusion *(māyā)* ? Kashmir Śaivism explains that the existence of this universe is just as real as the existence of Lord Śiva. As such it is true, real, pure, and solid. There is nothing at all about it which is unreal.

The fourth important difference between Kashmir Śaivism and Vedānta is that Vedānta does not recognize *kuṇḍalinī yoga*. The Vedāntins say that *kuṇḍalinī yoga* is meant for those

who are treading on the inferior path of yoga. From our
Kashmir Śaivaite point of view, however, *kundalini yoga* is
the most important yoga in this system. Kashmir Śaivism
explains that there are three ways of *kundalini yoga, parā
kundalini yoga, cit kundalini yoga,* and *prāna kundalini yoga.*
Parā kundalini yoga is supreme *kundalini yoga.* It is functioned by Lord Śiva with the universal body not the individual
body. *Cit kundalini yoga* is *kundalini* in consciousness. *Prāna
kundalini yoga* is *kundalini* in breath.

The fifth significant difference between Kashmir Śaivism
and Vedānta concerns the question of who is fit to practice this
monistic teaching. Vedānta holds that this teaching can only be
practised by "worthy" people such as Brahmins with good
qualities. In fact, Śamkarācārya holds that Vedānta is meant
only for *samyāsins*[1] and not others. From the Vedāntic point of
view women and other castes are not allowed to practise the
Vedāntic system. This point of view, however, is not recognized by our Kashmir Śaivism. Kashmir Śaivism teaches that
this monistic thought can be practiced by anyone, man or
woman, without the restriction of caste, creed, or color. In fact,
our Śaivism teaches us that this thought can be practised more
fruitfully by women than by men.[2]

---

1. Sanyāsins are "ascetics," those who have renounced all earthly concerns
   and have devoted themselves to meditation and the study of the
   Āranyakas and Upaniṣads, etc.

2. yoktāḥ saṁvatsarātsiddhiriha
   puṁsāṁ bhayātmanam |
   sā siddhistattvaniṣthānāṁ
   strīnāṁ dvādaśabhirdinaiḥ ||

   "That attainment which is said to be achieved in one years time by those
   terrified is achieved in twelve days by those divine ladies who are established in the true path of Śaivism."

   Quoted by Jayaratha in his commentary of Tantrāloka I

Kashmir Śaivism, therefore, is a universal system, pure, real, and substantial in every respect, which can be practiced by all.

Chapter Sixteen

The Seven States of Turya

The practical theory of the Seven States of *Turya* which is also known as the Seven States of *Ānanda* (bliss), and which I will now explain to you was taught to the great Śaivaite philosopher Abhinavagupta by his Master Śambhunātha.

Between the three states of the individual subjective body, waking, dreaming, and deep sleep, there is a gap. This gap is a junction. There is a junction between the waking state and the dreaming state. There is a junction between the dreaming state and dreamless sound sleep. And there is a junction between sound sleep and the waking state. This junction takes place automatically within every human being. Whenever you pass from wakefulness to the dreaming state you touch that junction and then enter into the dreaming state. Whenever you pass from the dreaming state to wakefulness you touch that junction first and then you open your eyes and experience the waking state. This state is touched whenever you pass between any of the three states of the individual subjective body. This junction is actually the fourth state, *turya*. This *turya*, however, cannot be experienced by gazing on this junction because whenever you gaze on this junction, waiting for the junction to happen, it will never happen. You will remain waiting in the waking state. It is when you fall asleep and enter into the dreaming state that you will find the junction. And yet ordinarily you remain absolutely unaware of the experience of this junction.

The only way to experience this junction is to concentrate on any center of the heart while breathing, while talking, or while moving here and there. You must concentrate on the center. You should watch the center of any two movements, any two breaths. You should concentrate on that junction. After some time when that concentration is established then whenever you go to bed to rest you will automatically enter the dreaming state through that junction. In this case though, you will not enter into the dreaming state. Instead, you will be aware at that point, at that junction. This junction is only a gate, the entrance to *turya*. Your awareness of this junction occurs only by the grace of your previous practice of centering your mind between any two movements or two breaths. This is the first state of *turya*. This state of *turya* is called *nijānanda*[1] which means "the bliss of your own Self".

You first experience that junction while practicing on any center such as the center which is found between any two breaths, or between any two movements, or between any two thoughts. When you concentrate in continuity with great reverence, with love, affection, and devotion, then your breath becomes very fine and subtle. Automatically you breathe very slowly. At that moment you experience giddiness. It is a kind of intoxicating mood. And when, during the experience of this giddiness, you do not destroy your alertness of concentration, this giddiness becomes firm and stable. This is the second state

---

1. nijānande pramatraṁśamātre hṛidi purā sthitaḥ

of *turya* known as *nirānanda*[2] which means "devoid of limited bliss." Here you do not lose awareness even though you feel intoxicated. And when that giddiness becomes stable and remains for a longer period then the aspirant falls asleep at once. Yet at this point he does not enter into the dreaming state, rather, he enters in that gap, that junction. This junction is known to be the start of *turya*. In entering this junction the aspirant enters into another world. It is not wakefulness, nor is it the dreaming state, nor is it sound sleep. This world is the fourth world. Here the organs of this aspirant do not function at all. He does not experience moving about nor does he hear or see. If, with great effort, he were to open his eyes he would feel that he is still sitting in his house, however, actually he cannot move any part of his body and can only slightly move his eyelids.

At that moment the aspirant hears hideous sound and sees furious forms. Those aspirants who are worried by these things try at once to come out from this state and after exerting great effort they come out and are again in the waking state. On the other hand there are those aspirants who try to tolerate these hideous and terrible things. For example, he may experience that the whole of the house has collapsed upon him, or he may experience that there is a fire burning outside and this fire will burn everything including himself. These experiences, if endured and tolerated, will pass away. If the aspirant cannot tolerate them then he will be thrown out into the waking state and must begin again. The aspirant, in order to continue his journey, must tolerate these hideous and terrible experiences. Here only one thing is predominant and must be maintained and that is breathing. The aspirant must breathe in and out with

---

2. śūnyatāmātravisrānternirānandaṁ vibhāvayet

devotion and great love towards his Self, which means breathing in and out while reciting the name of the Lord as he was instructed by his Master when he initiated him, all the while ignoring these terrible sounds. He may actually think that he is going to die, that he is really gone. These thoughts are wrong thoughts and he must ignore them. All of these experiences occur when the aspirant desires to move from individuality to universality because individuality has to be shaken off. When this movement towards universality begins this kind of struggle takes place.

If you continue with tolerance, breathing and internally reciting your mantra according to the instructions of your Master, then these terrible sounds and forms vanish and pulling and pushing in your breathing passage begins to occur. You feel as if you are choking and that you cannot breathe. This experience you must also tolerate. It will only vanish if you intensify your devotion for the Lord. You must insert more love and affection for your practice. If this is done then after some time this choking sensation will pass. If, however, at this point you do not intensify the devotion for your practice, then you will come out from this state and will need to begin again afresh. If this occurs you will feel foolish and realize that by not tolerating these experiences you have caused a great loss to yourself. Because of this you will be anxious to begin again.

This state of hideous sounds and forms followed by the sensation that you are choking and that your breathing is about to stop is called *parānanda*[3] which means "the *ānanda* (bliss) of breathing." When you breathe in and out with great divinity it is not ordinary breathing. Here your breathing becomes full of

---

3. prāṇodaye prameye tu paranandam vibhavayet

                                        Tantrāloka: V;45

bliss and joy even though you are experiencing terrible forms
and sounds or the fact that your breath is about to stop.

If you continue your practice with intense devotion in continuity your breath does stop. What happens is that at the center
of what is called in our Śaivism *lambikā sthāna*, which is
found on the right side near the pit of the throat, and in English
is known as the 'soft palate,' four passages meet. In ordinary
breathing two passages are open and two passages are closed.
When your breath is about to stop the passages of ordinary
breathing close. You experience this symptom when you feel
that you are choking and that your breath is about to stop. At
this point your breath becomes centralized and moves about
one point just like a whirlpool. The aspirant experiences that
his breathe is neither moving out or coming in. He feels that
his breath is moving round and round, that it is winding at that
one point which is the junction of the four passages. This state
is called *bhramānanda*[4] which means, "that bliss which is all
pervading."

Here the yogin must maintain the continuity of his devo-
tional practice. As his breathing has stopped and he cannot
watch his breath he can only recite mantras. He must put his
mind on his mantra and only his mantra with great devotion to
Lord Śiva. If he continues this practice with great devotion
then after some time yawning takes place or his mouth
becomes crooked just like at the time of death. These stages
are the same stages which take place when your breath has
stopped and you are about to die. The myriad changes that take

---

4. samānabhūmimāgatya brahmānandamayo bhavet

                                           Tantrāloka: V;47

"The equilibrium of breath, neither breathing in nor breathing out is brahmānanda."

place on his face are the changes that take place at the moment of death. The apprehension of death then arises in the mind of this yogī. He feels now that he is really dying. He is not afraid, he is apprehensive. This is the kind of death which takes place when individuality dies and universality takes birth. It is not a physical death it is a mental death. The only thing the yogī must do here is to shed tears of devotion. He must pray for the experience of universal "I." After a few moments, when the whirling state of your breath becomes very fast, moving ever more quickly, you must stop your breath at once. You must not be afraid. If your Master is there he will tell you at that moment to just stop your breath. This is because when there is the whirling of breath then there is the possibility that you may start breathing again. At this point it is in your hand to stop it or to let it go. When it has come to the extreme intensity of whirling then you should and must stop it at once!

When you stop your breathing then what happens next is that your breath immediately rushes down in the central vein. Your breath is "sipped" down and you actually hear the sound of sipping. The gate of the central vein *(madhyanāḍī)* opens at once and your breath reaches down the bottom to that place called *mūlādhāra* which is near the rectum. This state of *turya* is called *mahānanda*[5] which means, "the great bliss."

After *mahānanda* no effort is required by aspirant. From this point on everything is automatic. There is, however, one thing that the aspirant should observe and be cautious about and that is that he should not think that "everything is now automatic." The more he thinks that everything will be automatic the more surely he will remain at the state of *mahānan-*

---

5. udānavahnau viśrānto mahānandaṁ vibhāvayan

da. This is why Masters never tell the aspirant what will take place after *mahānanda.*

From the Śaiva point of view from *mahānanda* onwards, you must adopt *bhramavega.*[6] *Bhramavega* means 'the unknowing force.' Here you have to put your force of devotion without knowing what is to happen next. You cannot use your mantra because when your breath is gone your mind is also gone as the mind has become transformed into the formation of consciousness *(cit).* Here breathing takes the form of force *(vega).* It is this *vega* which pierces and penetrates *mūlādhāra cakra* so that you pass through it.

When the penetration of *mūlādhāra cakra* is complete then this force rises in another way. It is transformed and becomes full of bliss, full of ecstasy, and full of consciousness. It is Divine. You feel what you are actually. This is the rising of *cit kuṇḍalinī* which rises from *mūlādhāra cakra* to that place at the top of the skull which is known as *brahmarandhra.* It occupies the whole channel and is just like a bloom. This state, which is the sixth state of *turya,* is called *cidānanda*[7] which means, "the bliss of consciousness."

This force then presses the passage of the skull *(brahmarandhra)* piercing the skull to move from the body to the universe. This takes place automatically, it is not to be done. And when this *brahmarandhra* is pierced then at once you begin to breathe out. You breathe out once for only a second, exhaling from the nostrils. After exhaling everything is over

---

6. tāvadvai bhramavegena mathanam śaktivigrahe I
   bhedattu prathamotpannā vindavaste'tivarcasaḥ II
                           Tantrasadbhāva quoted in Śiva Sūtra Vimarśini

7. nirupādhirmahāvyākptirvyānākhyopādhivarjitā I
   tadā khalu cidānando yo jaḍānupabṛṁhitaḥ II
                                          Tantrāloka: V;49

and you are again in *cidānanda* and you again experience and feel the joy of rising which was already present. This lasts only for a moment and then you breathe out again. When you breathe out your eyes are open and for a moment you feel that you are outside. You experience the objective world, but in a peculiar way. Then once again your breathing is finished and your eyes are closed and you feel that you are inside. Then again your eyes are open for a moment, then they close for a moment, and then they again open for a moment. This is the state of *krama mudrā*, where transcendental "I" consciousness is beginning to be experienced as one with the experience of the objective world.

The establishment of *krama mudrā* is called *jagadānanda*[8] which means, 'universal bliss.' This is the seventh and last state of *turya*. In this state the experience of Universal Transcendental Being is never lost and the whole of the universe is experienced as one with your own Transcendental "I" Consciousness.

All of the states of *turya* from *nijānanda* to *cidānanda* comprise the various phases of *nimīlanā samādhi*. *Nimīlanā samādhi* is internal subjective *samādhi*. In your moving through these six states of *turya* this *samādhi* becomes ever more firm. With the occurrence of *krama mudrā*, *nimīlanā samādhi* is transformed into *unmīlanā samādhi* which then becomes predominant. This is that state of extraverted *samādhi* where you experience the state of *samādhi* at the same time you are experiencing the objective world. And when *unmīlanā*

---

8. yatra ko'pi vyavacchedo nasti yadviśvataḥ sphurat |
   yadanāhata-saṁvitti paramāmrita brimhitam ||
   yatrāsti bhāvanādīnāṁ na mukhyā kāpi saṁgatiḥ |
   tadeva jagadānanda ......||

   Tantrāloka: V;50-52

samādhi becomes fixed and permanent this is the state of
jagadānanda.

In terms of the process of the Fifteen Fold Rising the *sakala*
state is the waking state. *Sakala pramātṛi* is the first state of
turya, nijānanda. Vijñānakala[9] is the state of *nirananda.*
Śuddhavidhyā is the state of *parānanda. Īśvara* is the state of
brahmānanda. Sadāśiva is the state of *mahānanda. Śiva* is the
state of *cidānanda.* And *Parama Śiva* is the state of *jagadā-*
nanda.

There is a point twixt sleep and waking
Where thou shalt be alert without shaking.
Enter into the new world where forms so hideous pass;
They are passing—endure, do not be taken by the dross.
Then the pulls and the pushes about the throttle,
All those shalt thou tolerate.
Close all ingress and egress,
Yawnings there may be;
Shed tears—crave—implore, but thou will not prostrate.
A thrill passes—and that goes down to the bottom;
It riseth, may it bloom forth, that is Bliss.
Blessed Being, Blessed Being,
O greetings be to Thee.

Swami Lakshman Jee Brahmachari

---

9. From the state of *vijñānakala* the process of rising is automatic. Though
   there may be something to be done this something is neither physical or
   mental. Once the aspirant has attained the *vijñānakala* state he will never
   fall. If, for example, the aspirant once enters the state of *vijñānakala*
   between waking and sleeping, then during his lifetime he will never lose
   that state. Whenever he does his practice in continuity with devotion he
   will enter the *vijñānakala* state. This is because once the *vijñānakala*
   state has been experienced it leaves a permanent impression. At this point

you are not in the state of *pramātṛ* you are in the state of *vijñānākala*. *Vijñānākala pramātṛ* is much higher than the state of *vijñānākala*. *Vijñānākala pramātṛ* takes place after *śuddhavidyā*. The difference between *vijñānākala pramātṛ* and the state of *vijñānākala* is that the state of *vijñānākala* is ordinary while *vijñānākala pramātṛ* is special and more significant. This is also the case with all of the states and their *pramātṛns*. When you unknowingly experience a state then you are in that which is called a "state." When you knowingly experience any state, which means that you are active in that process, that is the state of *pramātṛ*. For example, when you enter in *samādhi*, you are not in the *pramātṛ* state of *samādhi*, rather you are simply in the state of *samādhi*. At this point you have no control over this state. You will enter into this state according to the choice of your Master or Lord Śiva. Sometimes you will wish to enter this state and you do enter it and sometimes you will wish to enter this state and yet you cannot enter it. You can be said to be in the state of *pramātṛ* only when you have the full authority of going to that state and returning from it whenever you will to do it.

Chapter Seventeen

Kuṇḍalinī and Its Purpose

Kuṇḍalinī śakti is the revealing and the concealing energy of Lord Śiva. On the one hand it is the revealing energy and on the other hand it is the concealing energy. It reveals and it conceals. This *kuṇḍalinī śakti* is not different from the existence of Lord Śiva, just as the energy of light and the energy of heat of fire are not separate from the fire itself. *Kuṇḍalinī*, therefore, in the true sense is the existence of Śiva. It is the life and glory of Śiva. It is Śiva Himself

In our Trika Śaivism *kuṇḍalinī*, which is that internal serpent power existing in the shape of a coil, is divided in three ways. The supreme *kuṇḍalinī* is called *parā kuṇḍalinī*. This *kuṇḍalinī* is not known or experienced by yogins. It is so vast and universal that the body cannot exist in its presence. It is only experienced at the time of death. It is the heart of Śiva. This whole universe is created by *parā kuṇḍalinī*, exists in *parā kuṇḍalinī*, gets its life from *parā kuṇḍalinī*, and is consumed in *parā kuṇḍalinī*. When this *kuṇḍalinī* creates the universe Śiva conceals His Real Nature and is thrown in the universe. When the universe is created He becomes the universe. There is no Śiva left which is separate from the universe. This is His creative energy. And when *kundalinī* destroys the universe Śiva's nature is revealed. So, the creative energy for the universe is the destructive energy for Śiva, i.e., it is the revealing energy for the universe and the concealing energy for Lord Śiva. And the destructive energy for the universe is the creative energy for Śiva. i.e., it is the concealing energy for the universe and the revealing energy for Lord Śiva.[1]

Parā kundalinī is the supreme *visarga* of Śiva. As you know from studying the theory of *mātṛikācakra*, *visarga* [:] comprises two points. These points are said to be Śiva and Śakti. In the real sense, however, these points are not Śiva and Śakti, they are the revealing point and the concealing point.

Cit kundalinī is experienced by yogins by means of concentrating on the center between any two breaths, two thoughts, or two actions, between the destruction and creation of any two things. As you have learned in your study of the Seven States of *Turya*, when the yogin maintains his awareness in continuity in concentrating on the center, he enters that junction which exists between any two states of the individual subjective body, waking, dreaming, or deep sleep. His breathing becomes coagulated then stops and whirls about one point. It then moves on the right side of the passage of the breath. If this yogin's awareness continues to be maintained in continuity, his breath is transformed from *prāna* (breath) into *prānana* (life) and it rushes down through the central vein which is on the right side[2] of the passage of the breath. It rushes down, to

---

1. When Lord Śiva is concealed He is in the state of *Anuttara Śiva*. When He is revealed He is then said to be in the state of *Maheśvara Śiva*.

2. There is only one vein through which the breath passes in the rise of *kundalinī*. When the breath is being sipped down it is sipped down on the right side and when it is returning it is in the center. The conception of iḍā, piṅgalā, and suṣumnā is a gross conception. It is only descriptive of

the bottom to the spot known as *mūlādhāra*, which is near the rectum. Then in *mūlādhāra* you briefly experience a crawling sensation. It is like the experience when a man and a woman are having intercourse and sexual climax is just about to take place. Here the beginning of intense pleasure takes place. After the momentary experience of this crawling sensation it rises again in one flash.[3] And when it rises you become filled with absolutely blissful existence. The happiness and bliss that you experience here just cannot be described. It is ecstasy beyond ecstasy. This bliss is just like sexual bliss. In comparing sexual happiness with the happiness experienced in *cit kuṇḍalinī*, however, you will find that sexual happiness is one millionth part of the happiness experienced in *cit kuṇḍalinī*. In addition, simultaneously with the experience of ecstasy you also realize the reality of Self. You recognize your Real nature and you know, "I am only bliss *(ānanda)* and consciousness *(cit)*."

And when you maintain that bliss through the grace of your Master then the force of *cit kuṇḍalinī* pierces *bhrūmadhya*, which is found between the eyebrows. At that point at once and abruptly you breathe out. Here you breathe out and not in and you do so only once. Once you breathe out your breathing is once again stopped. Then *cit kuṇḍalinī* rises from *bhrūmadhya* to *brahmarandhra*, which is found at the top of the skull. You experience the rising flow of *cit kuṇḍalinī* as filling the whole channel from *mūlādhāra* to *brahmarandhra*. Here again

---

the ordinary course of breathing. When *idā* is present then you breathe more from the right nostril. When *piṅgalā* is there then you breathe more from the left nostril. When *suṣumnā* is present then you breathe equally from both nostrils. *Idā*, *piṅgalā*, and *suṣumnā* have nothing to do with *kuṇḍalinī*.

3. sparśo yadvat pipīlikā

you abruptly breathe out and your eyes are open. This lasts for only a moment and then you are again inside without breathing, experiencing the rise of *kuṇḍalinī*. Then again you breathe out and again your eyes are open and for a moment you feel that the outside world is full of ecstasy and bliss. This happens again and again. One moment you are inside experiencing the bliss of the rise of *cit kuṇḍalinī* and then the next moment you breath out and your eyes are open and you are experiencing the world filled with ecstasy. This process of coming out and remaining in continues and each time it occurs it is filled with more and more ecstasy. This process is called *krama mudrā*.

When you are established in the process of *krama mudrā*, then you experience that ecstasy in action. When you eat you are in that bliss. When you talk you are in that bliss. When you walk you are in that bliss. Whatever you do you remain in that Universal state. This is the state of *jīvanmukti*, liberated life. This state is experienced not by ordinary yogins, this state is experienced only by great yogins. This is the real state of *cit kuṇḍalinī*.

In the actual rise of *cit kuṇḍalinī* you will only get a glimpse of it and then come out. The full rise of *cit kuṇḍalinī* takes place only by the grace of your Master and by the grace of your own strength of awareness. The experience of establishing the full rise of *cit kuṇḍalinī* through the process of *krama mudrā* can take place in one day, one life, or one hundred lifetimes.

Prāṇa kuṇḍalinī also comes about through the process of centering. *Prāṇa kuṇḍalinī*, however, is only experienced by those yogins who, along with their attachment to spirituality, also have attachments to worldly pleasures. If your desire and attachment is only for spirituality then *cit kuṇḍalinī* takes place. Whether you experience the rise of *kuṇḍalinī* as *cit kuṇḍalinī* or as *prāṇa kuṇḍalinī* depends on your attachments. If you have attachment for spirituality and also for worldly pleasures then the rise of *kundalini* takes place in the form of *prāna kundalini*. If you do not have attachments for worldly pleasures and are only attached to spirituality then the rise of *kundalini* takes place in the form of *cit kundalini*. There is nothing you can do to determine how the rise of *kundalini* will take place. It rises in its own way depending on your attachments.

Up to the point where your breath is sipped down in the central vein rushing to *mūlādhāra cakra* and through the momentary experience of the crawling sensation, the rise of *cit kundalini* and the rise of *prāna kundalini* are the same. In the rise of *prāna kundalini*, however, when the crawling sensation is finished, then in the state of *mūlādhāra* there is a *cakra* (wheel)[4] and this *cakra* begins moving forcefully with great speed in a clockwise direction. At the same time the yogin will also hear the sound of its movement.

After some time that force rises twelve finger spaces from *mūlādhāra cakra* to *nābhi cakra*, which is the *cakra* of the navel. When it reaches the navel then the *cakra* of the navel also begins to move and you feel that simultaneously two wheels are in movement and you feel the sound of that movement. Here, as in *cit kundalini*, the intensity of real love[5] blooms forth. It is so full of love and bliss that the experience of sexual bliss experienced at the height of intercourse completely pales in comparison.

---

4. In some *śāstras* it is said that these cakras contain lotus petals. In Śaivism these petals are not experienced nor are they recognized.

5. Love is the stuff of life. Without love you are not living. It is just as if you were dead. I am not speaking of sexual love, I mean real love. Real love exists in *kundalini*.

It is important for you to know that in the process of *prāṇa kuṇḍalinī* you may not go beyond *mūlādhāra cakra* or beyond *nābhi cakra*. You may only experience *mūlādhāra cakra* and then come out into the ordinary course of life. Then again you will have to begin with your practice of centering. For the full experience of *prāṇa kuṇḍalinī*, whether you are a householder, married or unmarried, you have to give your full life to it.

From *nābhi cakra* the force rises to *hrit cakra*, which is the *cakra* of the heart, and which is experienced as being right in the center in between the two breasts. When this force reaches *hrit cakra*, it also begins to move and you feel all three wheels moving with great velocity, you hear their sound, and you even experience the spokes that comprise their wheels. From *hrit cakra* the force of breath rises up to *kaṇṭhacakra*, the *cakra* of the pit of the throat, and this cakra also begins to rotate at a very high speed. From *kaṇṭhacakra*, the force of breath reaches to *bhrūmadhya cakra*, the *cakra* found between the two eyebrows, and it also begins to rotate. With the movement of *bhrūmadhya cakra* we have come to the end of the process of movement.

When the force of breath moves from *bhrūmadhya cakra*, rising to *sahasrāra cakra*, *sahasrāra cakra* does not begin rotating. It does not move, rather, it is pierced by great yogins. And this piercing does not always take place. Sometimes it is pierced and sometimes it is not pierced depending on whether or not you have attachment to universal pleasures. This piercing will only take place when you have no attachment at all for universal pleasures. And when you do pierce this *cakra*, then you become completely filled with bliss and enter into the process of *cit kuṇḍalinī*.

If you do not pierce this *cakra* then you will only travel up to *bhrūmadhya cakra* and from *bhrūmadhya cakra* you will come out and achieve *aṣṭasiddhiḥ*, the eight great yogic powers. These powers are *animā, laghimā, mahimā, garimā, īsitvam, vaśitvam, prākāmyam,* and *kāmāvasayitvam–vyāpti.*

Animā is the power of becoming invisible. *Laghimā* is the power to become so light that you can move through the air. *Mahimā* is the power to create and maintain, as Hanumān did, an enormous body. *Garimā* is the power to add weight to your body so that you become immovable. *Īsitvam* is the power to have control over the cosmos, e.g., you have the power to make it rain, or to make the sun shine. *Vaśitvam* is the power to make yourself attractive so that everyone wants to be with you. *Prākāmyam* is the power to have control over your own bodily system. *Prākāmyam* enables you to create hunger where there is none, or if you are hungry, to eliminate your feelings of hunger. The eighth power is *vyāpti* which is the power to pervade the whole universe. This power enables you to know what is occurring anywhere in the universe.

The danger inherent in these powers lies in the fact that when you have and use these powers then by and by you will be deprived of some portion of your spirituality. This occurs because, due to the charm of these powers, you become ever more devoted to worldly pleasures.

In Kashmir Śaivism there is a second way that *prāna kundalinī* may rise. Due to the bad luck of the yogī it sometimes rises in reverse. In the reverse rise of *prāna kundalinī,* when the breath is sipped down in the central vein and reaches *mūlādhāra cakra* you will find that *mūlādhāra cakra* is not moving. Instead you find that *bhrūmadhya cakra* is moving. In fact, what has happened is that the breath has crossed all of the *cakras,* beginning with *mūlādhāra cakra* and has reached and penetrated *bhrūmadhya cakra.* This *cakra* then begins to move. Then the force of the breath penetrates *kantha cakra* and it begins to move. Then the force of the breath moves to the heart, then to the navel, and finally reaches *mūlādhāra cakra* and all these *cakras* are in movement. Then you come out. The process of the reverse rise of *kundalinī* is completed.

This is the incorrect process of *prāṇa kuṇḍalinī*. It is called *piśācāveśah*, which means, "trance of ghosts."[6] It is a fruitless and valueless process. It only happens when your Master is not on good terms with you or is angry with you. He puts you in this process. In this reverse process you do not go anywhere or achieve anything. In fact, it leads you from right to wrong.

---

6. viṣayeṣveva saṃlīnānadho'dhaḥ pātantyanūn |
   rūdrāṇūnyāḥ samāliṅgya ghorataryo'parāḥ smṛitāḥ

   "These energies, which are the *ghoratarī* energies of Rudra, carry the individual downward by increasingly entangling him in the joy of the senses."

   Mālinī Vijaya Tantra: III;31

Chapter Eighteen

Variations in the Rise of Prāṇa Kuṇḍalinī

There are variations in the rise of *prāṇa kuṇḍalinī* from *mūlādhāra cakra* depending on the desires and longings of the aspirant. When a yogin has an intense desire and longing for achieving the recognition of Supreme "I" through the *mantra* '*aham*,' "I am," then, because of this desire and longing, his breath becomes full of bliss, joy, and ecstasy. Automatically this blissful force of breath penetrates *mūlādhāra cakra* in the form of this *mantra*. He feels simultaneously that he is the existence of, and one with, this rise of *kuṇḍalinī*. This sensation then moves and rises with the penetrating force of blissful breath from *mūlādhāra cakra* to penetrate *nābhi cakra*, which is found in the navel, from the navel to penetrate *hṛit cakra*, which is found in the heart, from the heart to penetrate *kaṇṭha cakra*, which is found in the throat, and finally from the throat to penetrate *bhrūmadhya cakra*, which is found between the eyebrows. This particular kind of penetration, brought about by the force of the *mantra* '*aham*,' "I am," is called *mantra vedha* in our Śaivism.

A different type of rising takes place when a yogin desires to uplift people. This yogin possesses this particular intensity of desire and feels that he is doing his practice just for the benefit of mankind. He does not want to help himself, he wants to help others. For him, the rise of *prāṇa kuṇḍalinī* begins with the blissful force of breath touching *mūlādhāra cakra* which then begins to move. Simultaneously the blissful force of breath is transformed into *nāda*. Here *nāda* means, "I am meant for the upliftment of mankind." Literally the word '*nāda*' means "sound." It is called *nāda* because this yogin wants to explain the Universal Reality to others. This sensation continues as *prāṇa kuṇḍalinī* rises to penetrate the navel, then the heart, then the throat, and finally the eyebrows. This particular type of penetration is called *nādavedha*.

The next variation in the rise of *prāṇa kuṇḍalinī* takes place when a yogin is attached to ease, comfort, happiness, and joy. He wants peace of mind and nothing else. In this case when the blissful force of breath in the form of *prāṇa kuṇḍalinī* penetrates *mūlādhāra cakra* and then rises to penetrate the navel, heart, throat, and eyebrows, it is transformed into a fountain of semen. He feels that it is a fountain of semen which is rising from *mūlādhāra cakra* to *brahmarandhra* and spreading throughout his body. It rises with tremendous force just like a fountain. How joyful and happy he becomes. Sexual joy is nothing in comparison. Due to the intensity of joy inherent in this particular rise of *prāṇa kuṇḍalinī* he loses all taste for worldly pleasures at once. This kind of penetration is called *binduvedha*.

Another variation in the rise of *prāṇa kuṇḍalinī* takes place when a yogin has the desire to become strong and to maintain his strength. He would like to maintain himself in perfect condition. He would like to be able to teach others concerning his internal feelings without experiencing any fatigue. In this person, when the blissful force of breath penetrates *mūlādhāra cakra* and then rises to penetrate the navel, heart, throat, and eyebrows, it rises in the form of an ant. This is because the blissful force of breath is transformed into energy. This is the rise of energy in *prāna kundalinī*. He feels that energy is being developed and that he is becoming the embodiment of energy. This particular type of penetration in *prāna kundalinī* is called *śākta vedha*.

The fifth variation in the rise of *prāna kundalinī* takes place when a yogin has the impression that the form and reality of *kundalinī* is actually serpent power. When the yogin has this impression then the rise of that blissful force of breath in the form of *prāna kundalinī* takes place in the form of a cobra. He actually experiences that it is a cobra which is rising with its tail remaining in and touching *mūlādhāra cakra* and stretching to penetrate all of the *cakras* up to and including *brahmarandhra*. This kind of penetration is called *bhujaṅgavedha*.

The sixth and last variation in the rise of *prāna kundalinī* takes place when the yogin acquires, in the course of his practice, the desire to secretly initiate a few of his disciples without anyone knowing. For this yogin, when the blissful force of breath penetrates *mūlādhāra cakra* and rises from *mūlādhāra cakra* to penetrate the navel, heart, throat, and eyebrows, it rises in the form of the buzzing of a black bee. He experiences the sound of a black bee and he also experiences the intense bliss associated with this rise. This type of penetration is called *bhramaravedha*.

Of these six variations of penetration which take place in the rise of *prāna kundalinī*, I would appreciate experiencing only two of them, *mantravedha* and *binduvedha*. I would give everything for the experience of these. Whether or not you experience a particular kind of penetration, however, is out of your hands. It is automatically determined by your deepest desires and longings.

Chapter Nineteen

Kashmir Śaivism

Kashmir Śaivism is known as the Pure Trika System. The word *"trika"* means, "the three fold signs of man and his world." In the thought of *trika* there are three energies, *parā* (supreme), *aparā* (lowest), and *parāparā* (combination of the lowest and the highest). These three primary energies represent the three fold activities of the world. In the thought of the Trika, therefore, it is admitted that this whole universe and every action in it, whether spiritual, physical, or worldly, is existing in these three energies.

The Trika Philosophy is meant for any human being without any restriction of caste, creed, or color. Its purpose is to enable you to rise from individuality to universality. The Trika System is comprised of four systems, the Pratyabhijñā system, the Kula system, the Krama system, and the Spanda system. These four systems, which form the one thought of the Trika system, all accept, and are based on, the same scriptures. These scriptures, which in Śaivism are called *āgamas*, are the ninety two *āgamas* of Śaivism, the monistic *Bhairava Śāstras* which are supreme *(parā)* and which are 64 in number, the mono-dualistic *Rūdra Śāstras* which are medium *(parāparā)* and which are eighteen in number, and the dualistic *Śiva Śāstras* which are inferior *(aparā)* and which are ten in number.

Pratyabhijñā System

The word *pratyabhijñā* means, "to recognize, to realize your Self spontaneously once again." Here you have only to realize, you do not have to practice. There are no *upāyas* (means) in the Pratyabhijñā system. You must simply recognize who you are.

Wherever you are, whether you are at the level of Supreme Being, at the level of yoga, or at that level which is disgusting, you can recognize your own Nature there and then without moving anywhere or doing anything. For example, take the case of a bride and bridegroom. The woman has not seen her husband to be and craves to see him. Concerning him she has only heard praise and glory but she has not actually met him. Suppose this girl and her future husband by chance happen to go separately on the same pilgrimage. When they arrive at the place of pilgrimage they meet. The girl, however, does not feel any importance in this man because she does not know him to be her future husband. Yet her future husband and this man are the same person. Later, when a friend introduces her to him telling her that this is the man who is to be her husband then she is filled with happiness, pleasure, and ecstasy. She realizes that this is the same man she had seen before.[1] In the same

---

1. taistairapyupayācitairupanata-
   stamvyāḥ sthito'pyāntike
   kānto lokasamāna evam-
   aparijñāto na rantuṁ yatha I
   lokasyaiṣa tathānavekṣitaguṇah

way reality dawns in the Pratyabhijñā system. In which ever level you are situated do not mind. The moment recognition *(pratyabhijñāna)* dawns not only do you instantaneously become divine, but you also realize that you were already divine. At that moment you realize that you were already the Lord but did not know it because you had misunderstood yourself.

In the Pratyabhijñā philosophy it is your Master who tells you that you are the same person for which you are longing and teaches you to reach the goal there and then without adopting any means. This teaching, therefore, is situated chiefly in *anupāya*, which is that means where there are no means at all. It is the recognition that there was nothing to be done and nowhere to go. Here there is no practice, no concentration, no meditation. By the grace of your Master you realize it and you are there.

The Pratyabhijñā System was flourishing in the beginning of *Kali yuga*. As time passed, however, it became veiled due to misunderstanding. It wasn't until the end of the eighth century A.D. that the great Master Somānanda reintroduced the Pratyabhijñā System in Kashmir. Somānanda's disciple was Utpaladeva, and his disciple was Lakṣmaṇagupta, and his disciple was the very great Abhinavagupta.

Kula System

The Kula System teaches you how you can live in *caitanya* (Universal Consciousness), the real nature of yourself, in both

---

svātmāpi viśveśvaro
naivālaṁ nijavaibhavāya
tadiyaṁ tatpratyabhijñoditā ||

Īśvarapratyabhijñā Kārikā: IV;2

the ascending and the descending act. While you rise from the lowest to the highest you realize your nature, and while you descend from the highest to the lowest you realize your nature. In the Kula System there is no break in the realization of your own nature either in the highest circle or in the lowest circle. This system, therefore, teaches you how you can live in totality.[2] In fact, the word *kula* means "totality."

In the practice of the Kula System you have to realize the totality of the universe in one particle. Take one particle of any thing which exists in this world. In that one particle is to be realized the totality of the whole universe. The totality energy is found in one particle. Everything is full of one thing and one thing is full of all things.[3]

The difference between the Pratyabhijñā System and the Kula System is only that the Pratyabhijñā System teaches you how to realize your own nature in one place and exist there, reside there, while the Kula System teaches you how you can rise from the lowest degree to the highest degree and all the while experience the nature of your Self on the same level and state. Śiva, which is realized in *prithvī tattva* is the same level, the same reality of Śiva which is realized in *Śiva tattva*. Here there is complete realization in every act of the world.

---

2. Totality does not mean where there is only knowledge and not ignorance or where there is only ignorance and not knowledge. Totality is that state where knowledge and ignorance exist together, when there is knowledge there is ignorance and when there is ignorance there is knowledge. Both knowledge and ignorance are digested in the totality, nothing is excluded.

3. ekaikatrāpi tattve'pi ṣaṭtriṁśattattvarūpatā

   "In any one element you will find all of the thirty six elements."

The Kula System was introduced in Kashmir in the beginning of the 5th century A.D. by Śrīmacchandanātha. Later, in the 9th century, because its teachings had become distorted, it was reintroduced by Sumatinātha. In the line of Masters that followed from Sumatinātha, Somanātha was his disciple. Śambhunātha was the disciple of Somanātha, and the great Abhinavagupta was the disciple of Śambhunātha.

Krama System

The Krama System does not recognize either the ways of the Pratyabhijñā System or of the Kula System. In the Krama System you have to rise step by step in succession. This system teaches that step by step realization makes your realization firm. As the Krama System is concerned with successive realization it is primarily concerned with space and time because where there is succession there you will find the existence of space and time. In both the Pratyabhijñā System and the Kula System you are beyond space and time. In the Krama System it is in the end, not in its process, that you are beyond time and space because it also carries you to that timeless and spaceless state.

The Krama system is primarily attributed to *śaktopāya* and to the twelve *kālīs*. The twelve *kālīs* are said to be the twelve movements of any one cognition. For example if you look at any object such as a pot, the sensation travels from your thought to the place of the pot and then returns again from the place of the pot to your thought giving you the sensation whereby you realize this pot. You do not realize this pot at the place of the pot, you realize this pot in your mind. Your perception has moved from inside to the pot and then returned again from the pot to your thought. And these movements are distributed in twelve ways as the twelve *kālīs* in the Krama System.

The rise of *prāṇa kuṇḍalinī* is also described in the Krama System because in *prāṇa kuṇḍalinī* you rise from one *cakra* to another *cakra*, from one state to another state. As this is a successive process it is found in the Krama System.

Although the Krama System existed in the beginning of *Kali yuga*, having been introduced by the sage Durvāsā, it was reintroduced at the end of the 7th century A.D. in Kashmir by the sage Erakanātha who was also known as Śivānandanātha. Śivānandanātha had only three chief disciples which he initiated into the Krama System and all three were females, because in this system predominance is given only to *śakti*.[4] Their names were Keyūravatī, Madanikā, and Kalyāṇikā. They were quite prominent and were completely informed in the Krama System. Afterwards these ladies also initiated disciples which were both male and female.

Spanda System

The fourth system which comprises the Trika philosophy is called the Spanda System. The word *spanda* means "movement" and the Spanda School recognizes that nothing can exist without movement. Where there is movement there is life and where there is no movement that is lifelessness. They realize that there is movement in wakefulness, dreaming, deep sleep, and *turya*. Though some thinkers argue that there is no movement in deep sleep, the philosophers of the Spanda System realize that nothing can exist without movement.

The teachings of the Spanda System, which is an important practical system, are found embodied in the *"Vijñāna*

---

4. In this system you will find Tantras where Pārvatī initiates Śiva and Śiva becomes the disciple.

Bhairava Tantra," the *"Svacchanda Tantra,"* and in the 6th
chapter of the *"Tantrāloka."*

The Spanda System was introduced in Kashmir by the great
sage Vasuguptanātha in the beginning of the 8th century A.D.
Vasuguptanātha is the author of both the *"Śiva Sūtras"* and the
"Spanda Kārikās."[5] The disciple of Vasuguptanātha was
Kallaṭa.

---

5. Some teachers think that the *"Spanda Kārikās"* were not composed by
   Vasuguptanātha, instead they were composed by his disciple Kallata.
   This theory, however, is absolutely wrong.